OWL

PRACTICAL

PRINCE2

Colin Bentley

London: TSO

TSO

Published by The Stationery Office and available from:

The Stationery Office
(mail, telephone, fax & email orders only)
PO Box 29, Norwich NR3 1GN
General enquiries/Telephone orders 0870 600 5522
Fax orders 0870 600 5533
E-mail book.orders@tso.co.uk
Textphone 0870 240 3701

You can now order books online at www.tso.co.uk

The Stationery Office Bookshops
123 Kingsway, London WC2B 6PQ
020 7242 6393 Fax 020 7242 6394
68–69 Bull Street, Birmingham B4 6AD
0121 236 9696 Fax 0121 236 9699
9–21 Princess Street, Manchester M60 8AS
0161 834 7201 Fax 0161 833 0634
16 Arthur Street, Belfast BT1 4GD
028 9023 8451 Fax 028 9023 5401
18–19 High Street, Cardiff CF10 1PT
029 2039 5548 Fax 029 2038 4347
71 Lothian Road, Edinburgh EH3 9AZ
0870 606 5566 Fax 0870 606 5588

The Stationery Office's Accredited Agents
(see Yellow Pages)

and through good booksellers

First edition Colin Bentley copyright 1998
Second edition The Stationery Office copyright 2002

ISBN 0 11 702853 3

Printed in the United Kingdom by

CONTENTS

1 OVERVIEW

1.1 Purpose and benefits

A project is considered successful if it is completed on time, within budget and the end product meets the required quality. These good things are not achieved by luck or by simply working hard. They need a method, an approach that will work time and time again for projects of any size. PRINCE2 helps do this by ensuring at the start that everyone involved knows what the project's objectives are, what the steps are to get there, and who is to do what. It then provides checks at key moments to ensure the four targets are being achieved – time, budget, functionality and quality.

PRINCE2 is a lot of common sense, the amalgam of a lot of lessons learned the hard way about what can go wrong in a project and how a project can be structured to either avoid or give early warning of most common failings. Following on from its two predecessors, PROMPT II and PRINCE, PRINCE2 is the result of over twenty-five years' development effort and the experience of hundreds of years of project managers' work.

Many projects have proved that the PRINCE2 method works. Its use is free. It is continually improving. Where PRINCE version 1 was aimed at IT projects, PRINCE2 can be applied to any kind of project. It makes a lot of sense for a company to use one project management method for all its projects. This avoids reinventing the wheel. Management understands the project structure, the roles, the plans, the controls. It knows what reports to expect and the format of the reports. Staff can move from one project to the next and feel on familiar territory.

Finally, a number of companies and government departments are now preferring sub-contractors who use PRINCE2 in their projects. Thus, there seem to be many benefits in using PRINCE2.

1.2 The fundamental principles of PRINCE2

A project should be driven by its Business Case.

A project exists in a customer/supplier environment, i.e. the customer and supplier will have different cost-centres and may have separate Business Cases.

A project should have clearly defined roles, established at the outset of the project. The roles should include some means of assuring senior management of the correct functioning of the project within its constraints, a means which is independent of the Project Manager.

Every project should begin with work to define:

■ what is required

■ why the effort is justified

- who is involved and in what capacity
- how a solution will be developed
- when the various products of this solution will be developed.

A project should be broken down into a number of stages, commensurate with its size and risk exposure, to allow senior management representatives to review progress at the end of each stage before committing to the next stage.

1.3   The composition of PRINCE2

PRINCE2 is built around:

- a set of processes which provide a flexible framework of steps to manage the project
- a number of components, which are used by the processes and explain the PRINCE philosophy and approach
- a small number of techniques which support the processes
- descriptions of a number of management products which will be useful in the project.

Figure 1.1 gives an impression of how these parts of PRINCE2 support each other.

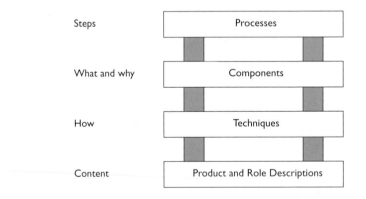

Figure 1.1

1.4   The PRINCE2 processes

There are eight processes:

■ Starting up a Project	(Gathering basic information)
■ Initiating a Project	(Getting agreement that we know what we are doing)
■ Controlling a Stage	(Day-to-day monitoring and control)
■ Managing Product Delivery	(Controlling development)
■ Managing Stage Boundaries	(Taking stock and getting ready for the next part of the project)
■ Planning	(Common planning steps)
■ Closing a Project	(Making sure the project has done the job)
■ Directing a Project	(Senior management taking decisions at key points of the project)

1.5   PRINCE2 components

The components of PRINCE2 cover:

- ■ Business Case
- ■ Organisation
- ■ Control
- ■ Plan
- ■ Quality
- ■ Management of Risk
- ■ Configuration Management
- ■ Change Control.

1.6   PRINCE2 techniques

There are only three techniques:

■ Change Control	(A technique for capturing, processing and tracking all changes and questions)
■ Product-based Planning	(A method of planning based on identifying the products which have to be delivered)
■ Quality review	(A team method of checking the quality of a document)

PRINCE2 also offers descriptions of each role which might be needed in a project (these need tailoring for each specific project) and Product Descriptions of the purpose and content of the management products of a PRINCE2 project.

And that's it. That is all there is to PRINCE2. It does not try to cover every facet of project management. Skills and techniques, such as network planning and team motivation, which are well covered in other literature, are not touched. PRINCE2 works comfortably alongside such techniques. The various elements of PRINCE2 merge and link with one another to provide a comprehensive project management method which is strong yet flexible, powerful without being bureaucratic.

2 PROCESSES

The eight processes in PRINCE2 document the project management steps that should be considered for any project. They cover the work of the Project Board (the DP process), the Team Manager (the MP process) and the Project Manager (the remaining processes). In small projects a process may take only a few minutes. In a large project a process such as Controlling a Stage (CS) may be repeated over a period of months or years. The amount of time and effort needed for a process depends on the individual project.

Figure 2.1 relates the processes to the creation of the PRINCE2 management products.

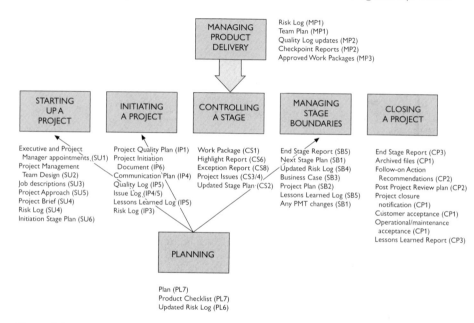

Figure 2.1

2.1 Starting Up a Project (SU)

This is a pre-project process. It is triggered by the Project Mandate. Only enough work is done to ensure that the products required to ask for authorisation to begin initiation are present.

2.1.1 Aim

The process aim is to establish:

- who the decision makers are to be
- what (in general terms) the product to be delivered is

- why the project should be done
- how we will go about providing a solution
- what the expected quality is
- a log to record risks
- how much effort it will take to plan the project.

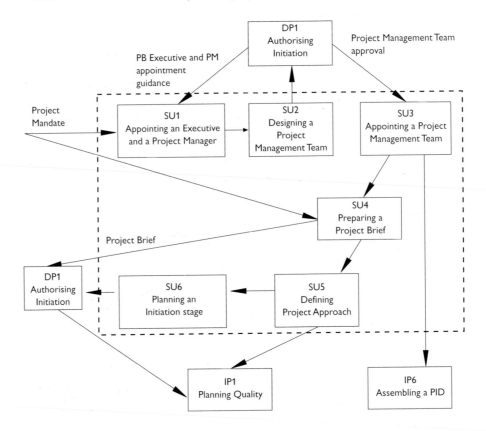

Figure 2.2

2.1.2   Appointing a Project Board Executive and a Project Manager (SU1)

A project is triggered by the delivery of a Project Mandate. Now we need someone to work on it and someone to make decisions. It is normally corporate or programme management who make these appointments. For very small projects that are not part of an overall strategy, a project sponsor may appoint himself or herself to be the Executive.

The steps are very simple:

- identify the Executive from the project's stakeholders or sponsors

- identify a suitable Project Manager

- confirm their availability

- agree job descriptions for them

- appoint them to their roles.

2.1.3   Designing a Project Management Team (SU2)

This process should be read in conjunction with the Organisation component. The aim is to decide who else should be on the Project Board, who will carry out any Project Assurance duties, whether the Project Manager needs any administrative support, and whether any Team Managers will be needed.

Its aim and steps appear very simple, but there are a number of questions that should be asked. A mind map and text of these questions are given in Figure 2.3.

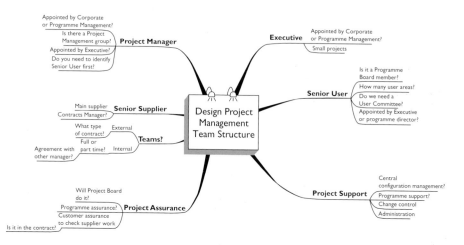

Figure 2.3

2.1.3.1   Executive

This is really part of the SU1 sub-process, but it is worth checking. If the project is part of a programme, has someone from programme management taken the role of Executive? This will give a highly motivated leader for the Project Board, but may limit the Executive's time available to this project. This may influence the choice of how business assurance needs to be handled.

If it is a small project and the sponsor has appointed himself or herself as Executive (or the Project Manager has 'appointed' the Executive), it is worth checking that the project subject is not part of a higher strategy, in which case the Executive should have been appointed by programme management.

2.1.3.2   Project Manager

Again this is really part of SU1. But it is worth verifying whether the Project Manager appointment came from programme management or just from the Executive. If the project is part of a programme, this means that there will be many interfaces with other projects for the Project Manager to handle, therefore make sure that someone with the right level of competence has been chosen.

Should the Senior User be appointed before choosing the Project Manager? Might the Senior User want a say in the choice of Project Manager?

Does the organisation have a project management support group? If so, what is the relationship between the Project Manager and that group? What support is available from the group? How will their involvement be managed? Will there be a role for them as part of Project Support or Project Assurance?

2.1.3.3   Senior User

If the project is part of a programme, the programme management has the power to appoint people to this role. Has this appointment already been made? Is the Senior User a member of the programme management?

How many user areas are there which might wish to propose someone as a Senior User? For example, have you considered branch office users as well as head office users? Have any proposed people got the necessary authority to be decision makers?

If there are many user areas, how will you keep the number of Senior Users to a sensible number? Should you suggest a User Committee that is represented by a Senior User?

2.1.3.4   Senior Supplier

Who is providing the development resources? In-house or external? If there are several external teams, do you need all of their companies represented on the Project Board? Could one main supplier act as Senior Supplier and be responsible for the commitment of the others? This will probably only work where the sub-contractors are under contract to the main supplier, rather than direct to you. If there is no main supplier, but lots of small contractors, could your contracts/procurement manager fill the role of Senior Supplier? Remember that the Senior Supplier is accountable for the quality of what the teams deliver. If the supplier is external, make sure that someone of adequate authority is appointed who can ensure that the right level of quality is provided.

2.1.3.5   Project Assurance

Will the Project Board members carry out their own assurance?

If the project is part of a programme, is there a programme assurance group that will require a role in the Project Management Team?

A key part of the user assurance role is to check the quality of supplier work, starting with checking the supplier's plans and adding quality checks and checkers to those plans. If you are using external suppliers, is this requirement in the contract? If not, it may be difficult to enforce.

2.1.3.6   Teams

If they are external, what type of contract do you have with them? What are its stipulations about reporting, liaising with Project Assurance, negotiation on Work Packages?

If the teams are internal, is the staff allocated full-time or part-time to the project? If part-time, is there a solid agreement with their manager about the division of their time?

2.1.3.7   Project Support

Will configuration management be provided from a central specialist group?

If part of a programme, is there any programme support that will give assistance?

Is there any central or programme group to provide change control expertise and co-ordination?

Does the project need administrative help?

Do you need expert help with any project management tools, such as planning and control software, risk analysis tools?

2.1.4   Appointing a Project Management Team (SU3)

It is essential that everyone involved in the project understands and agrees:

- who is accountable for what
- who has what authority
- who is responsible for what.

Having designed the Project Management Team, the task in this sub-process is to agree the job descriptions in writing. It is sensible to start with the standard role descriptions available in PRINCE2 and tailor these to be specific to the project.

It is wise to get two copies of the agreed job description signed by the person concerned. They keep one. The other is filed by the Project Manager. At the end of each stage the Project Manager should confirm whether there is to be a change to the management team for the next stage, e.g. a change in the Project Assurance roles. If there is any change to a member of the Project Management Team, this sub-process should be repeated for the change.

2.1.5   Preparing a Project Brief (SU4)

The Project Brief is the main input document to project initiation and forms the basis of the Project Initiation Document. In a perfect world, whoever triggers the project will provide a Project Brief. It is not a perfect world, so the aim of this sub-process is to turn the Project Mandate (over which we had no 'official' control) into the Project Brief. If the project is part of a programme where all projects are being run under PRINCE2, then it is possible that the Project Mandate will, in fact, be a full Project Brief, and there will be no work to do here.

Apart from the Project Brief, another product should be created at this time, the Risk Log. This needs to be created here because the first risks are likely to be found in the Project Mandate or when turning this into the Project Brief.

The Project Brief will contain pieces of information which affect many later products and processes. Its terms of reference will form the basis of the Project Initiation Document. It will contain the customer's quality expectations, which will affect the Project Quality Plan. It should contain some justification for the project that can be revised into a full Business Case as part of the initiation process. It forms the basis of the Project Board's decision (DP1) on whether to approve the move into initiation.

An article written by Patrick Mayfield and myself (but mainly Patrick) provides a lot of understanding about the role of the Project Brief and its relationship with the Project Mandate and Project Initiation Document. A copy of the article is reproduced here (from section 2.1.5.1 to section 2.1.6, not including Figure 2.6).

2.1.5.1   Why bother with the Project Brief?

A key product at the start of a project is the Project Brief. It is clear from talking with many in the PRINCE community that the real power in this product can be easily overlooked. A common initial reaction is, 'You mean we have to have a Mandate, then a Brief, and finally a Project Initiation Document … and all before we can proceed with the project?!'

Truly, this can seem like over-engineering the whole business of controlling the start of a project. But is it?

2.1.5.2   The Project Mandate

Let us first review the nature of the Mandate. It is helpful to refer to Figure 2.4.

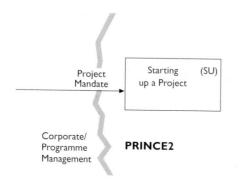

Figure 2.4

The thick grey line represents the start of the PRINCE2 process – its 'domain', if you will. So we see that the Project Manager does not 'write' the Mandate. In fact, the inclusion of the Project Mandate's Product Outline is one of the most controversial parts of the PRINCE2 manual; it suggests the Project Manager does write it. Not so.

Ultimately, the Project Manager must accept the Project Mandate, in whatever form it comes, however incomplete it may be. In fact, in a typical business situation the Project Mandate will be scrappy. Knowing this, the designers of PRINCE2 developed the concept of a Project Brief.

2.1.5.3   So is the Project Brief an outline Project Initiation Document?

One *could* consider it this way. However, the authors of PRINCE2 chose not to call the Project Brief an outline Project Initiation Document (PID) since the Project Brief is not supposed to cover the complete scope of the eventual PID. The emphasis is much more on getting crucial project aims confirmed quickly, rather than outlining the complete control environment.

Figure 2.5 shows the evolution from Project Mandate to Project Brief to PID. At each transition, the scope may widen, but each document draws on information from its predecessor. It is envisaged that whilst the Project Mandate might be nothing more than a memorandum, and where the PID might be a set of documents in a ring-binder, the Project Brief would still be *brief*.

Figure 2.5

2.1.5.4 So is the Project Brief just a cut-down Project Definition?

No, definitely not. It has the potential to be rather more than that.

Consider the very nature of a project. It is about making beneficial change. Thus a project should be in essence an act of creation. As all creators know, a creation is always created twice: first in the mind of the creator and second in actuality. Since PRINCE2 deals with that class of projects where a team of people are involved, the first creation – the vision of that future beneficial state – needs to be clearly communicated within the team … and at the earliest possible point.

This is where the Project Brief can yield great benefit.

The Project Manager, or perhaps the Executive, will want to define effectively the vision for the project. This person will want to set clearly the whole direction of the project by casting this vision outwards and downwards to the rest of the project team as well as upwards to corporate management for confirmation and approval.

The Project Brief can help this process by in effect containing the vision statement for the project.

2.1.5.5 How can the Project Brief state a project's vision?

In the composition of the Project Brief the authors suggest elements such as:

- project objectives
- project scope
- outline project deliverables and/or desired outcomes.

Some practitioners have looked at the words 'project deliverables' and have read no further. They have described the purpose of the project in terms of a list of deliverables or products. To be sure, this always has been one of the great strengths of PRINCE in helping all concerned to focus on the end products.

However, in terms of 'casting the project vision' PRINCE2 allows the Project Manager to go further. One client using PRINCE2, for example, has described the desired outcomes in terms of 'a day in the life of a user' at the end of the project, a sort of pen portrait or storyboard. It describes in one short paragraph within the Project Brief how their working practices might be changed for the better by what the project would deliver.

This has enormous power in generating an early debate between the supplier and the customer about what the broad aims, purposes and scope of the project really are. It can be couched in non-technical language, and is at such a high level that it need not prejudice later detailed specification work.

The result of the Project Brief is that a vision is clearly shared, the team's expectations are aligned and the project can be initiated on a much clearer basis.

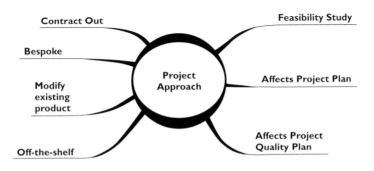

Figure 2.6

2.1.6 Defining Project Approach (SU5)

Although this process is the fifth sub-process, it will need to be done in parallel with creating the Project Brief in SU4, and may affect the design of the Project Management Team. The options are shown in Figure 2.6 and the impact discussed.

2.1.6.1 Feasibility study

The project may have been brought about by a feasibility study. As part of the study, a number of solution options will have been considered. The justification for the project may be based on the costing given in the feasibility study for the adoption of that solution. This means that the Project Approach will be based on the accepted solution proposed by the feasibility study. This would mean that there is little or no work to be done in this sub-process, other than to confirm that the recommended solution is still valid and matches the cost side of the project justification.

2.1.6.2 Contract out

One possible Project Approach is to contract the work out to an external group. This can provide instant expertise and experience in areas where the customer is lacking. It also gives a solution without having to take on permanent staff. The contractor handles all the detailed planning and staffing headaches, leaving the Project Manager to set progress and quality controls and monitor against these.

The tricky part of this approach is how to monitor the quality of the contractor's work, in particular during the development. The answer is to ensure the involvement of the customer's Project Assurance in the contractor's planning and work.

2.1.6.3   Bespoke

This means developing a new solution with in-house staff. It increases the Project Manager's planning and control load, compared with contracting the work out. It may bring in problems such as training, staff or contract worker hire, working in new areas of specialisation, using new tools. Cost control now becomes much more of a problem for the Project Manager, but quality is under more direct control.

2.1.6.4   Modify existing product

It may be a shorter task to take an existing product and modify it to meet the new needs. This may be the product currently being used by the customer, but other options include products that are being used by other departments or companies.

There are a number of concerns about this approach. It may not be the cheap option it seems. Have a look at the product in question. How modifiable is it? Will you end up with a revised product that is maintainable and enhanceable? Is the structure of the existing product good enough to cope with major modification?

In the past some companies have asked for an off-the-shelf product to be modified to suit their needs. But later they have got into problems with keeping the product in line with future enhancements to the standard package and have found themselves with no one left on the providing company's staff who understands their modified version. Take, for example, the purchase of a car. If a production-line car is chosen, then modified to be exactly what is required, the warranty will probably be nullified. Any repairs needed may need special expertise, modified parts, take an abnormally long time to do, and so on.

2.1.6.5   Off-the-shelf

This is a very popular and normally cheap option. It also has the benefit of being immediately available, regularly updated with new or improved features and has a proven track record. The major work for such a project is to modify other products and processes that have to interface with the new product.

It is, however, very difficult to operate a normal type of change control mechanism if problems are found with the product, and the power of the customer to get requests for change implemented is very small. Such requests are competing with the requests of all other users of the product. Even if they are accepted, the cycle of change may not be what the project wants.

2.1.6.6   Affects Project Plan

The Project Approach affects the Project Plan. The choice of contracting, new development, modification or purchase of an off-the-shelf solution will have a major impact on time frame and cost. The type of specialist resources needed will also be affected. Training in a new off-the-shelf product, for example, will come much earlier in the project than with a bespoke product. In the first case, it is the 'developers' who need training in the product before tailoring the surrounding products and processes. In the latter case it is the users who need training after the product has been developed.

2.1.6.7   Affects Project Quality Plan

The choice of an off-the-shelf product will have a major impact on, for example, the Project Quality Plan. The types of test possible, their timing and the resources needed will be different from those for a bespoke product. There is seldom the opportunity to take part in the testing of the product as it is being built. The types of test may be different to those normally used. On the other hand, much of the basic testing will have been done, and the selling company may have access to lots of problem 'work-arounds' which have been used by its existing customer base.

2.1.7   Planning an Initiation Stage (SU6)

When the Project Brief is presented to the Project Board, the hope is that it will authorise the work to create the Project Initiation Document. Part of the philosophy of 'management by exception' is that all work is authorised before it is done. This means that when the Project Manager asks for authorisation to create the Project Initiation Document, he or she must tell the Project Board how much time, effort and cost this will take. So one of the products presented to the Project Board is the Initiation Stage Plan.

Other products developed or checked during start-up will affect this. The Project Approach may affect the amount of work needed during initiation. The Project Brief will indicate how much effort will be needed to refine the Business Case and risks.

2.2   Initiating a Project (IP)

PRINCE2 recommends that there should always be an initiation stage for any size of project. The Project Board's authorisation to move into the initiation stage (DP1) is the 'official' start of the project, where the Project Board and the Project Manager confirm in writing their understanding of what is to be done, what constraints apply, and how the project is to be controlled.

2.2.1   Aim

Draw up a 'contract' (the Project Initiation Document) which formally states:

- what key products the project will deliver
- why there are good reasons for doing the project
- the scope of what we are doing
- any constraints which apply to the product we are to deliver
- any constraints which apply to the project
- who is to be involved in the project decision-making
- how and when the products will be delivered and at what cost
- how we will achieve the quality required
- what risks we face
- how we are going to control the project
- what is the next commitment we are looking for.

2.2.2   Planning Quality (IP1)

This is done once for the whole project. It takes in the customer's quality expectations and the Project Approach from the Project Brief. These are matched with any quality standards that the customer and/or the supplier has. Then the Project Quality Plan is written to define in general detail what standards will be used. It may be sufficient to point at a quality management system (QMS) which exists and say that the project will meet those requirements. Additionally the Project Quality Plan should state any allocation of quality responsibilities. For example, is there a role for anyone from an independent quality assurance group? Is there some senior manager outside the project in the supplier's organisation who has overall responsibility for quality?

Each stage will provide details of who will do the checking and when. These should reflect the general statements made in the Project Quality Plan. The Project Quality Plan should include statements of how configuration management and change control will be done, including responsibilities for these.

A blank Quality Log should be setup. This will keep details of every quality check planned and done.

2.2.3   Planning a Project (IP2)

The Project Plan is an essential part of the Project Initiation Document. It tells the Project Board how long and how much it will take to develop the end product(s). It also explains what types and numbers of resources will be needed. This is essential information before the Project Board decides whether to commit to the project or not.

Input

Output

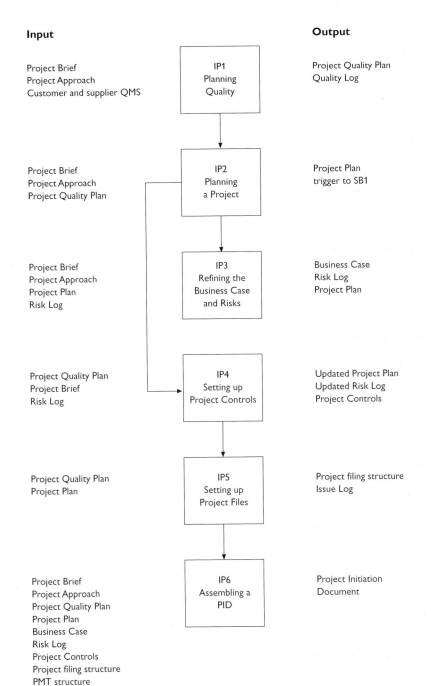

Project Brief
Project Approach
Customer and supplier QMS

IP1
Planning
Quality

Project Quality Plan
Quality Log

Project Brief
Project Approach
Project Quality Plan

IP2
Planning
a Project

Project Plan
trigger to SB1

Project Brief
Project Approach
Project Plan
Risk Log

IP3
Refining the
Business Case
and Risks

Business Case
Risk Log
Project Plan

Project Quality Plan
Project Brief
Risk Log

IP4
Setting up
Project Controls

Updated Project Plan
Updated Risk Log
Project Controls

Project Quality Plan
Project Plan

IP5
Setting up
Project Files

Project filing structure
Issue Log

Project Brief
Project Approach
Project Quality Plan
Project Plan
Business Case
Risk Log
Project Controls
Project filing structure
PMT structure

IP6
Assembling a
PID

Project Initiation
Document

Figure 2.7

The Project Plan is also a major control document for the Project Board. Apart from the initial commitment, it is studied at the end of every stage to compare actual progress with what was originally estimated and to judge whether the project is still in line with its original targets. The initial Project Plan stays unchanged in the Project Initiation Document, but a revised version of it will be produced at every end stage to show actual dates and costs achieved and any revised target dates and costs.

All PRINCE2 plans have the same format. The development of all PRINCE2 plans uses the common Planning (PL) process.

2.2.4   Refining the Business Case and Risks (IP3)

The Project Mandate should have contained some business reason for the project. By the time this was changed into the Project Brief, there should have been a basic Business Case. This may have just been reasons or it may have included some actual costs and financial evaluations of expected benefits. The details may have come from earlier work, such as a feasibility study. These need checking to see if the figures are correct and up to date. Sometimes the feasibility study may be months old. Sometimes further work on the terms of reference reveals that the figures given in the original Business Case are based on incorrect assumptions or calculations.

For most projects at this time, the Business Case should have a cost-benefit analysis done, to show the Project Board how much needs to be invested in order to gain savings or new benefits, both expressed in financial terms.

The Risk Log may have included some known risks stated in the Project Brief. As the Project Initiation Document is developed, more risks may come to light. The Project Plan may throw up new risks or need to be modified to reflect actions to be taken to counter risks. New information may come to light about risks already in the Risk Log.

The Project Approach may contain risks or change existing risks.

Risk countermeasures may also affect the project costs, and therefore the Business Case.

2.2.5   Setting Up Project Controls (IP4)

This defines what monitoring, reporting and control mechanisms are needed by the Project Management Team. It should be divided into what is needed to support:

- Project Board control
- Project Manager control
- (where appropriate) Team Manager control.

Details of the PRINCE2 controls can be found in the Control component.

Products input to this sub-process are the Risk Log and the Project Quality Plan. The Risk Log will impact on the Project Board's choice of how many stages the project should have, i.e. how short it wishes to keep its forward commitment before assessing the risk situation again. The requirements of the Project Quality Plan may affect the composition of Work Packages. The required flow of information to and from all stakeholders should be identified and assembled in a Communication Plan.

Some PRINCE2 users prefer to put the arrangements for configuration management and change control in this section.

2.2.6   Setting Up Project Files (IP5)

It is important to keep a record of some things; why decisions were made, approvals given, agreements on actions, who did what. There may be a disagreement between customer and supplier or between Project Board and Project Manager, where it is necessary to go back and find out either what was agreed or why something was done.

Project files should be set up in such a way to facilitate information retrieval and audit.

Among the files to be set up is the Issue Log. This records details of all issues raised once the Project Initiation Document has been agreed.

Another product created here is the Lessons Learned Log, used to jot down any good or bad experiences during the project. It should cover the management processes and techniques. Optionally it can also hold experiences about any specialist tools and techniques. At the end of the project it is turned into a report.

A suggested project filing system is given in Appendix C.

2.2.7   Assembling a Project Initiation Document (IP6)

The objective of this sub-process is very simple – to collate the Project Brief and all the information gathered or refined in the earlier IP sub-processes into the Project Initiation Document, the 'contract' between Project Board and Project Manager on:

- what the project is to do
- why the project is needed
- who is accountable and responsible for what
- how it is to be done
- how it is to be monitored and controlled
- when the key products will be delivered.

This document is one of the two required by the Project Board as input to the sub-process Authorising a Project (DP2), the other being the plan for the next stage.

2.3   Controlling a Stage (CS)

This process handles the day-to-day management of a stage by the Project Manager. It is triggered by the Project Board sub-process Authorising a Stage or Exception Plan (DP3).

2.3.1   Aims

- Allocate work to individuals and/or teams
- Check on progress
- Ensure that the quality is satisfactory
- Ensure that changes are controlled
- Report on progress
- Watch for plan deviations
- Keep an eye on the risk situation
- Watch for anything that would impact the Business Case.

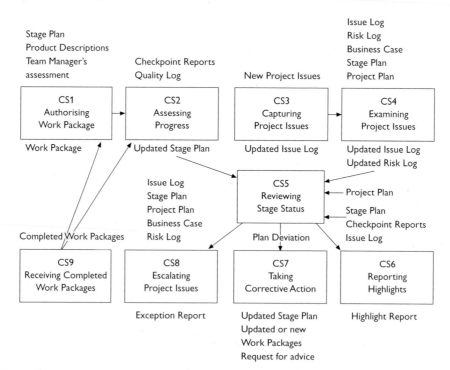

Figure 2.8

2.3.2   Authorising a Work Package (CS1)

An essential part of a Project Manager's control of a stage is that he or she knows who is working on what products. In order to achieve this, all new work must be allocated and approved by the Project Manager.

Combined with the allocation should be agreement on what progress feedback there should be. This may be in the form of timesheets (individuals) or Checkpoint Reports (teams).

Another part of the allocation should be details of how, against what quality criteria, by whom and at what points in the development of the product(s) the quality should be checked. The first two come from the Product Description(s). The last two will either come from the Stage Plan or, if appropriate, be built into the Team Plan. In both cases there should be the participation of the Project Assurance function in defining who should be involved and when.

Product development is authorised in Work Packages, containing the Product Description, performance and reporting expectations and, if useful, the relevant extract from the Stage Plan.

The basic philosophy behind the sub-process is that the Project Manager will negotiate details of a Work Package with a Team Manager. But it works equally as well, if more informally, with an individual in projects where there is one team, which works directly for the Project Manager. It is the choice of the Project Manager to allocate Work Packages for each single product or combine a number of products in one package. The former gives more control, but requires more frequent meetings. Where dealing with an external supplier it may be more convenient for both parties to put several products in the same Work Package.

2.3.3   Assessing Progress (CS2)

This sub-process covers the gathering of progress information, including examination of the Quality Log to check on the status of quality checking work. The progress information may come from timesheets and/or Checkpoint Reports.

The Stage Plan is updated with the information. This is one of the products which will be examined in Reviewing Stage Status (CS5).

2.3.4   Capturing Project Issues (CS3)

This sub-process is a useful partner to Assessing Progress (CS2) in gathering information for the Project Manager. It covers the work of ensuring that any issues, questions, potential changes or problems are documented and put in the Issue Log. The sub-process is, therefore, part of the change control procedure.

A suggested format for a Project Issue is given in Appendix F of this book.

Where a project is big enough or important enough to warrant it, the work here may be delegated to a member of Project Support, ideally a configuration librarian.

2.3.5   Examining Project Issues (CS4)

This covers the impact assessment of Project Issues. There are two sides to impact assessment: technical impact and business impact.

Technical impact covers assessment of how much work would be involved in making the necessary changes, the cost of this work and when it could be scheduled. Part of this is finding out how many products would be affected. This information would be held by the configuration management system. The senior specialists of the project normally do technical impact assessment. This 'extra' effort should be remembered when scheduling their work.

Business impact covers the assessment of any impact on the Business Case and risks of the project. This impact could, of course, be good as well as bad. Whoever is responsible for business assurance should be involved in the assessment of any business impact.

2.3.6   Reviewing Stage Status (CS5)

In a medium or large project, the work of sub-processes CS2, CS3 and CS4 may have been delegated, but this process is the key stage control point for the Project Manager. It brings together the progress information, the Quality Log and the Issue Log to be compared with the Stage and Project Plans and their tolerances.

This sub-process will happen many times in a stage. Figure 2.9 explains the Project Manager's work at this time.

2.3.6.1   Quality Log

Is the planned quality checking being done? Are team members or external contractors excluding quality checks to save time? What were the results of the quality checks? Does the quality of products look good or bad? Are discovered errors being cleared up quickly? Are the methods of quality inspection effective, or are errors being discovered later?

This is one place where an independent quality assurance representative would get involved (as part of Project Assurance).

Where one or more teams of external contractors are doing work, this check is very difficult to do. Project Assurance can help by identifying resources to be involved in the team's quality checking.

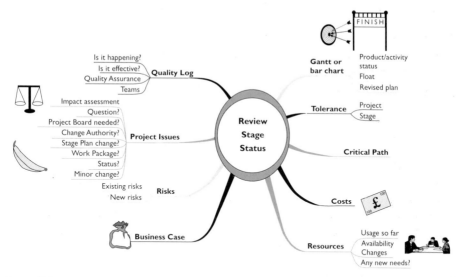

Figure 2.9

2.3.6.2   Project Issues

What should happen to any new issues? Do any need allocating for impact assessment? Are there any missing impact assessments which should have been done? Are there any impact assessments done and awaiting decisions? What issues are questions that can be handled immediately? Are there any minor changes that could be made within the current Stage Plan? Should any of this work be authorised by the Project Manager, or should they all be sent to the Project Board for prioritisation? Have change decisions been invested in a change authority? Should the Stage Plan be modified because of the Project Issue? Should one or more new Work Packages be authorised? What is happening about authorised changes?

2.3.6.3   Risks

What is the status of existing risks? Are all risks being monitored? When was the last update? Do the new Project Issues contain new risks, or impact on existing risks? Should I add risk monitoring tasks to my Daily Log for the next few days?

2.3.6.4   Business Case

Are the accumulating costs affecting the Business Case? Do the latest Stage Plan actuals impact on the Business Case? Do any of the open issues contain a threat or potential benefit to the Business Case?

2.3.6.5   Gantt or bar chart

Have those products been completed which were expected to be complete? Has work expected to start actually started? Are any unfinished activities going to extend beyond their expected end date? If there are any schedule problems, are they within their float? Does the Stage Plan need revision?

2.3.6.6   Tolerance

Is there a trend in time or money expenditure that threatens to go outside the tolerance margins? Has any information come to light that would affect the project tolerances, possibly in a later stage?

2.3.6.7   Critical path

What is the status of activities on the critical path? Should anything be starting or finishing on the critical path in the next few days?

2.3.6.8   Costs

Is the feedback information allowing me to keep an accurate check on expenditure?

2.3.6.9   Resources

Do I have details of usage so far? Has the availability of any resource changed? Have any new needs surfaced which will require extra resources?

The Project Manager has to assess whether the stage is on schedule and likely to finish within the tolerances. There are a number of possible reactions:

- Everything is progressing satisfactorily. Check if any new Work Packages should be authorised (CS1).
- Some deviation has occurred. Corrective action (CS7) can be taken within tolerance margins without referring to the Project Board.
- It can now be forecast that either the stage or the project will deviate beyond its tolerances in spite of what actions the Project Manager might take. This will trigger escalation of the problem to the Project Board (CS8).

2.3.7   Reporting Highlights (CS6)

When approving progress into the stage, the Project Board sets a requirement on the Project Manager to report on progress at a certain frequency. The frequency will vary according to such factors as the length of stage and the risk situation. It is normally set for all stages in the Project Initiation Document, but it is possible for the Project Board to vary the frequency stage by stage. Receipt of this control report is part of the Project Board's management by exception. It can be used as an early warning of a problem, which, if not solved, would lead to a deviation beyond tolerances.

The formal name for this progress report is the Highlight Report. A suggested format is given in Appendix B and a template for it is in Appendix F to the book. The Highlight Report is a consolidation of the information in the Checkpoint Reports from the team(s).

2.3.8   Taking Corrective Action (CS7)

This covers minor modifications to the Stage Plan (within tolerances) to react to deviations or new work. It may trigger new Work Packages (CS1) or modify existing ones. One reaction to an activity in trouble would be to swap resources around.

The sub-process may include an informal request to the Project Board for advice. The advice received may allow the Project Manager to carry on or may force the production of an Exception Report (CS8).

2.3.9   Escalating Project Issues (CS8)

A core part of management by exception is that the Project Board knows that a stage will not deviate beyond the tolerance margins it has set without an early warning of this being given by the Project Manager.

This sub-process gives that early warning. The Project Manager gives an Exception Report to the Project Board, defining the problem, the available options, a recommendation and a survey of the impact on Project Plan, Business Case and risks.

The Project Issue that causes the escalation may be a Request For Change. It may be a group of change requests, rather than just one. The Exception Report may be saying, 'If you want these extra changes, I am going to need more time and money.' It may be an off-specification, where the Project Manager reports that he or she is failing in some technical, financial or temporal way to deliver what the customer wants.

The Exception Report is input to the sub-process Giving Ad Hoc Direction (DP4).

2.3.10   Receiving Completed Work Packages (CS9)

This is a simple sub-process to match Delivering a Work Package (MP3). The Project Manager acknowledges receipt of completed and approved products from a team or individual. The Stage Plan is updated. The Project Manager records any useful comments in the Work Package about the performance of the team or individual. Other checks are that the completed products have been properly lodged with the configuration management system and that the relevant Quality Log entries are up to date.

2.4   Managing Product Delivery (MP)

The purpose of this process is to set down the basic steps for a Team Manager to manage the interface between an external team and the Project Manager. The philosophy can be used in an informal manner in situations where the interface is between the Project Manager and an individual working directly for the Project Manager.

The process is required irrespective of whether the team comes from an external supplier who does not use PRINCE2.

2.4.1   Aims

■ Negotiate details of the Work Package with the Project Manager

■ Do it

    ☐ Plan it

    ☐ Allocate it to team members

    ☐ Keep track of progress

    ☐ Report progress

    ☐ Make a record in the Quality Log of quality checks carried out

    ☐ Control changes

■ Give it back.

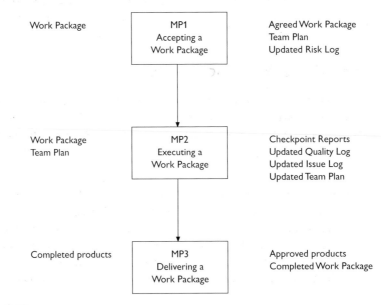

Figure 2.10

2.4.2   Accepting a Work Package (MP1)

The principle here is that the Project Manager should not simply allocate work to a team (or an individual) without discussion. There should be negotiation and agreement by both parties that the Work Package is reasonable and achievable. Elements of this agreement are:

- what is to be delivered
- target dates (and cost if this is relevant)
- what constraints and tolerances apply
- with whom there must be interaction
- reporting arrangements and frequency
- how and from whom approval for the products of the Work Package is to be obtained.

Also this sub-process covers the production of a Team Plan for the work. As with other plans, this includes risk analysis. Any new risks should be added to the project's Risk Log so that the Project Manager is aware of them.

Part of a Work Package should be a Product Description for each product to be made. The Team Manager should check that the quality criteria and quality method are usable and adequate.

When producing the Team Plan, this should be done in co-operation with those with Project Assurance responsibilities, identifying key quality checking events and resources to be involved in these. Those with Project Assurance responsibilities may come from both the customer and the supplier.

2.4.3   Executing a Work Package (MP2)

This is a smaller version of Controlling a Stage (CS). The Team Manager allocates the work to team members and monitors and controls against the Team Plan. Checkpoint meetings are held at intervals defined in the Work Package and Checkpoint Reports sent to the Project Manager. The Team Manager has to update the Quality Log with details of quality checks done.

If the Team Manager believes that the agreed time tolerances will be broken, the Project Manager must be informed immediately. The Exception Report format can be used, although it is the Project Manager's decision on whether the report is sent to the Project Board. It may be possible to handle the problem within the stage tolerances. Handling cost tolerances depends on the contract that exists between the team and the project. For example, if it is a fixed-price contract, this may have to be dealt with by the supplier.

2.4.4   Delivering a Work Package (MP3)

The sub-process has three parts:

- Obtain approval for the products developed from the person or group identified in the Work Package
- Hand over the approved products (for example, to the configuration librarian). Again, this should have been defined in the Work Package
- Advise the Project Manager of completion of the Work Package.

It may also be that something occurred during the work which should be recorded in the Lessons Learned Log. If so, the Project Manager should be given details.

2.5   Managing Stage Boundaries (SB)

At the end of each stage the Project Manager prepares a status report for the Project Board plus a plan for the next stage.

The steps of this process are also used when an Exception Plan is needed.

2.5.1   Aims

- Gather the results of the current stage
- Plan the next stage
- Check the effect on
  - ☐ the Project Plan
  - ☐ the Business Case
  - ☐ the risks
- Report and seek approval.

2.5.2   Planning a Stage (SB1)

The main objective here is to plan the next stage of the project. The high level summary of the next stage is expanded from the Project Plan into sufficient detail that the Project Manager will be able to control progress against it on a day-to-day basis. The Planning (PL) process is used to develop the plan.

A Stage Plan should include all products, not only the specialist ones, but management products as well. Typical management products would be Highlight Reports and the next Stage Plan that will require preparation towards the end of the stage. Quality activities and products should also appear in the plan. Whoever is providing Project Assurance should be

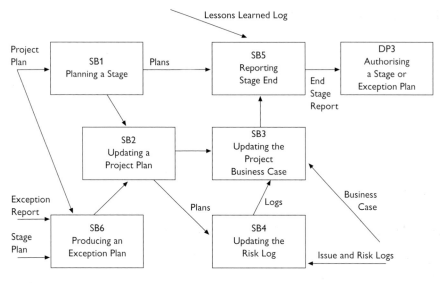

Figure 2.11

consulted about the timing and resourcing of quality activities before the Stage Plan is presented to the Project Board.

The Project Management Team structure should be checked for changes and any new job descriptions prepared.

2.5.3   Updating a Project Plan (SB2)

The Project Quality Plan and Project Approach are checked for any changes necessary to reflect the current status of the project. Any changes will form a basis for updating the Project Plan.

The Project Plan is updated based on:

■ the actual costs and times from the current Stage (or Exception) Plan

■ the new detail of activities and costs from the next Stage Plan (unless there is no next Stage or Exception Plan)

■ any other acquired knowledge about the project.

The last might be information about changes which have been agreed by the Project Board and which will cause activities in the next Stage Plan.

The Project Manager should describe in the End Stage Report (or Exception Report) why any change to the Project Plan has occurred.

2.5.4   Updating a Project Business Case (SB3)

The objective is to review the costs, benefits and timings stated in the current version of the Business Case, and create a new version if changes have occurred. Various factors will affect this process including:

- the final implementation date of the project may have changed, which might affect some or all of the benefits
- the cost of delivering the end products might have changed, thus affecting the cost-benefit analysis figures
- approved changes will have affected products, costs, times and benefits
- the environment into which the end product will be delivered may have changed
- the situation with regard to external suppliers may have changed.

2.5.5   Updating the Risk Log (SB4)

This sub-process represents one of the formal moments in a project when the risks in the Risk Log are reviewed to see if their status has changed.

Planning of the next Stage Plan or an Exception Plan may have raised new risks or change existing risks. This sub-process should therefore be carried out in conjunction with the sub-process Analysing Risks (PL6).

Updates to the Project Plan and Business Case earlier on in this process may have made changes that affect items in the Risk Log.

2.5.6   Reporting Stage End (SB5)

The results of the current stage are presented in an End Stage Report, which includes the actual results of the stage in terms of effort expended, costs, products produced and their delivery dates. These are compared to the original Stage Plan (or approved Exception Plan). Performance against the agreed tolerances for the stage is measured, and a report is given of the quality control activities undertaken and the results of that work.

A summary is given of all Project Issues received during the stage, the cumulative figures for the project, and the current status of all issues.

The next Stage Plan, a revised Project Plan, Business Case and Risk Log accompany the End Stage Report. The report identifies any variations from the previous versions of these products and assesses the impact of any changes against the original Project Initiation Document. If the project is still viable in the Project Manager's view, a request to proceed to the next stage will accompany the End Stage Report.

Any lessons learned during the stage are added to the Lessons Learned Log. Any lessons from the current stage are summarised in the End Stage Report.

2.5.7   Producing an Exception Plan (SB6)

Although this is the sixth sub-process, this does not mean that it is done last. If needed at all, it replaces Planning a Stage (SB1), and should be supported by the other sub-processes (SB2–SB5).

If a stage or the project is forecast to go outside the tolerances agreed with the Project Board when the plan was approved, and the situation cannot be rectified, the Project Manager has no further authority to carry on with the work. The Project Board must be advised of the situation at the earliest possible moment and asked for a decision.

The Exception Plan will have been triggered by the Project Board from process Giving Ad Hoc Direction (DP4), following receipt of an Exception Report from the Project Manager. An Exception Plan has the same structure as other PRINCE2 plans and, like other plans, is created using the Planning (PL) process. It will normally run from the present time to the end of the stage. However, if it is the Project Plan that is in exception, a revised Project Plan should be created, taking into account the actuals to date. A revised Project Plan would have to be referred by the Project Board to corporate or programme management, the people who set the project tolerances in the first place.

2.6   Closing a Project (CP)

The process covers the Project Manager's work to wrap up the project either at its planned end or premature close.

One of the fundamental features of any project is that it is finite – it has a defined start and end. The processes Starting Up a Project (SU) and Initiating a Project (IP) helped us to define the start of a project. This process helps us bring the project to a controlled close. The actual project closure has to be done by the Project Board, as explained in sub-process Confirming Project Closure (DP5), but this process prepares the necessary inputs to that.

A clear end to the project is more controllable than drifting into operational management. It is formal recognition by customer, supplier and those who will support the end product in its useful life that the operational support is ready to take over, or that the products from this project are ready to feed into some subsequent project or larger programme.

Closing a project provides a useful opportunity to:

■ take stock of project management performance and experience

■ ensure that all unachieved goals and objectives are identified, so that they can be addressed in the future.

Preparation for closing the project is triggered from sub-process Reviewing Stage Status (CS5) when the approaching end of the final stage of the project is detected.

All the CP processes may be done in parallel or at least with considerable overlap.

The method of 'Closing a Project' has to be tailored to suit the needs of the particular project. If the project has delivered an intangible product, for example to bring about a change in philosophy, then the objective of ensuring operation and support arrangements are in place may not be appropriate.

The following is an illustrative list of aims of the process to close the project. According to the type of project, they may not all be required.

■ Ensure that all expected products have been handed over to and accepted by the customer

■ Ensure that arrangements for the support and operation of project products are agreed

■ If the project has been closed prematurely, document what has been achieved and recommend the way forward

■ Identify any recommendations for follow-on actions

■ Document any lessons resulting from the project

■ Prepare an End Project Report, assessing the project's performance against the Project Initiation Document

■ Plan any Post Project Review required

■ Notify the host location of the intention to disband the project organisation and release resources.

There may be a number of Project Issues that were held over by the Project Board. These may lead to new projects or enhancements to the product during its operational life. The Project Manager records these appropriately in a document, Follow-on Action Recommendations.

The Lessons Learned Log, which has been developed during the project, is now organised into a Lessons Learned Report.

Suggested contents of the management products described in this process can be found in Appendix B.

2.6.1   Aims

■ Check everything has been delivered

■ Check that the end product is accepted

■ Make sure there are no loose ends

■ Store the project records for audit

■ Release resources.

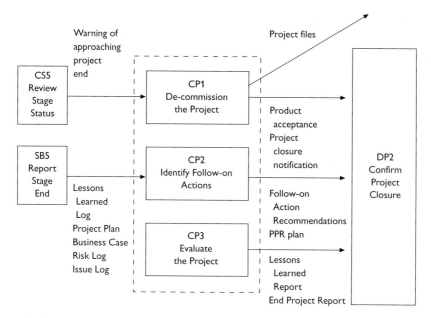

Figure 2.12

2.6.2   De-commissioning a Project (CP1)

The objectives of the sub-process are to:

- ensure that all project products have been approved and handed over to the customer

- confirm that the correct operation and support environment is in place (where applicable)

- confirm that the delivered products meet any needs defined for operation and support (where applicable)

- warn everyone who has provided support for the project of its close, so that they can plan for the return of the resources provided for that support

- complete and store all project information.

The Project Manager prepares the project closure notification to the host location that the project resources and the support services can be disbanded, but this has to be confirmed by the Project Board.

Before closure of the project can be recommended, the Project Manager must be assured that the expected results have all been achieved and delivered (or have been told by the Project Board that the project is to be closed prematurely).

Where a product has to be supported and sustained during its useful life, there must be confirmation in the report by the groups that will support the product that they have received the product in a state that allows them to carry out their duties.

To permit any future audit of the project's actions and performance, the project files should be archived. The files should include a copy of all the management products created during the 'Closing a Project' process.

2.6.3   Identifying Follow-on Actions (CP2)

The fundamental principle here is that if there is any unfinished business at the end of the project, it should be formally documented and passed to those who have the authority and responsibility to take action. The input will come mainly from those Project Issues that were put into 'pending' status by the Project Board during the project.

The aims of the process, therefore, are to:

■ document all unfinished work as Follow-on Action Recommendations

■ recommend a date and plan for any Post Project Review(s) considered necessary.

The quality, effectiveness and achievement of benefits claimed for the project products in the Business Case should be reviewed after a period of use. Examination of the latest version of the Business Case will identify when the expected benefits can be measured. The Project Manager should make a recommended plan for a Post Project Review, showing:

■ the benefits to be measured

■ the measurements to be applied

■ the skills required to perform the measurements

■ when the measurements can be taken.

2.6.4   Evaluating a Project (CP3)

Successful organisations learn from their experiences with projects. This is more likely if the lessons learnt are somehow preserved beyond the end of the project and disseminated to other projects.

Warning: This does need the identification and staffing of some central group to whom the responsibility is given to act as the focal point for these lessons. This may be a quality assurance group or project management support group.

The objectives of this sub-process are to:

■ assess the performance of the project and quality management against what they were intended to achieve .

■ identify lessons to be learned from the project and applied on future projects.

2.6.4.1   End Project Report

The Project Manager documents in the End Project Report how well the project has performed against its Project Initiation Document.

Any benefit achievement or non-achievement that can be defined by the time of project closure should be part of the report. The report should also take into consideration the effect of any changes that were approved.

The End Project Report should provide statistics on changes received during the project and the total impact of approved changes.

2.6.4.2   Lessons Learned Report

At the start of the project a Lessons Learned Log was created. A note should be added to this every time any member of the Project Management Team spots something in the management, specialist or quality processes and procedures which either made a significant contribution to the project's achievements or caused a problem.

In this sub-process all the notes in the log should be correlated and turned into a report. The report is also the repository of any useful measurements and quality statistics collected during the project that will help in the planning and estimation of subsequent projects.

2.7   Planning (PL)

The PRINCE planning philosophy is that:

- plans are constructed by identifying the final products required, their prerequisite products, and then the activities, their sequence and appropriate resources needed to deliver these products
- plans should cover management needs as well as the specialist products
- there should be assurance that all quality activities are planned in advance and to a level consistent with the control requirements identified in the Project Initiation Document.

This product-based approach to planning can be applied to any type of project. The steps are:

- establishing what products are needed
- determining the sequence and dependencies of each product
- identifying what activities are necessary to provide these products.

The steps involved are the same for all levels of plan, and several iterations of the planning process are normally needed.

2.7.1   Aims

A checklist of the aims of the process would be:

- identify and verify the objectives
- ascertain if there are any constraints
- think about how you're going to do the work
- what product(s) must be produced?
- what product(s) will you need in order to do the work?
- how will you check the product quality?
- in what sequence must you do things?
- what progress reports will be needed?
- what resources will you need?
- what assumptions are you making?
- what risks are involved?
- how many grey areas or unknowns are there?
- what tolerances would be reasonable?

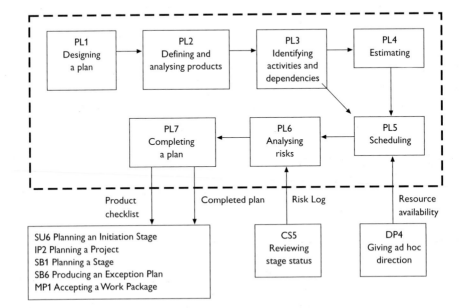

Figure 2.13

2.7.2   Designing a Plan (PL1)

This sub-process is needed only once, near the start of the project as a precursor, for example, to producing the Project Plan. This is where choices are made on the planning tools, estimating methods, levels of plan and monitoring methods to be used for the project. All recipients of plans and their updates are identified.

2.7.2.1   Planning tools

Any planning and control tools to be used by the project are identified. There may be a company standard or the customer may stipulate the use of a particular set of tools. The choice of planning tool may in part, however, depend on the complexity of the project.

The Project Quality Plan and Project Approach chosen for the project are prerequisites for designing a plan. They should have been defined as part of the process Starting Up a Project (SU).

According to the size and complexity of the project the next decision is the number of levels of plan required. Only the Project Plan and Stage Plans are mandatory. The scale of the project, its level of risk and the extent of control required will dictate the number of levels of plan.

The Plan component describes the PRINCE2 concept of plan levels. The identification and selection of stages is discussed in the Control component.

2.7.2.2   Estimating

The method of estimation and any estimating tools to be used must be chosen. A note should be put in the Lessons Learned Log about the accuracy of the estimating methods and tools as experience grows in their use.

2.7.2.3   Change budget

A budget to cover the cost of any anticipated changes to the initial requirements may have to be considered for inclusion when planning.

2.7.2.4   Change authority

The Project Manager and the Project Board must agree how to cater for funding changes to requirements. The basic process is to produce Exception Reports to ask the Project Board for extra money to cover the implementation of Requests for Change, but it can be difficult to find the necessary amount of Project Board time if it has to be done frequently. If the environment suggests that there will be many changes during the project it is sensible to discuss with the Project Board whether there should be a change budget. If so, consideration must be given to how this should be handled and by whom when producing the plans.

2.7.3   Defining and Analysing Products (PL2)

This sub-process is the start point for every PRINCE2 plan. It is divided into three steps:

- identify the specialist and management products to be produced
- produce a Product Description for each product, including its quality requirements, and ensure that these descriptions are fully understood and agreed by everyone involved
- put them in their logical sequence.

These steps are described in more detail in the Product-based Planning technique.

2.7.4   Identifying Activities and Dependencies (PL3)

Having identified the required products, the activities needed for the creation and delivery of each of the products need to be identified to give a fuller picture of the plan's workload.

The sub-process is divided into three steps. As with the other Planning sub-processes, there are likely to be several iterations:

- identify all activities necessary to produce and deliver the products
- establish the interdependencies between activities
- ensure that any internal and external dependencies to the project are covered.

Management activities should be included as well as the activities needed to develop the specialist products.

2.7.5   Estimating (PL4)

The objective of this sub-process is to calculate the resources and time required to complete each activity. This will include not only people, but also all other types of resource that will be required.

A Project Plan will normally require top-down estimating (i.e. an estimate for the total project, broken down across the stages for the project), whereas a Stage Plan would use bottom-up methods (an estimate for each product or activity, built up into a figure for the whole stage).

The major steps in a typical estimating process are:

- identify resource types required

  Identify the skills required for the project by type and experience. Requirements may include non-human resources, such as equipment, travel, and money. At Project Plan level it may be enough to state the skill types required. For lower level plans the resources should be identified by name.

■ estimate effort required for each activity

The estimated resource effort can now be added to the activity list. (At this point the estimates will be provisional estimates.)

The reliability of estimates depends on:

■ understanding the products (from the Product Descriptions)

■ how good and detailed the understanding of the activities is

■ any assumptions made.

The assumptions should be recorded in the plan's text. This information will enable the Project Board to set appropriate tolerances. Tolerances are fully described in the Control component.

It is best to use a group of people who are experienced in both estimation and the subject of the project. Use of a number of people tends to balance out any individual over-optimism or pessimism in estimation.

Where possible, estimating should include discussion with the people who will be responsible for doing the work.

When resources have been estimated it may become clear that resource constraints cannot be met. If this should happen, the matter should be referred to the Project Board.

2.7.6   Scheduling (PL5)

The objectives of scheduling are to:

■ allocate suitable resources to the identified activities

■ schedule the activities according to the sequence and dependencies defined in sub-process PL3

■ smooth resource usage within the bounds of any identified dependencies, spare time (float) and any external time constraints

■ identify any additional resource effort needed and negotiate with the Project Board to resolve this

■ calculate total requirements for human and other resources and produce a cost for the schedule.

There are many different approaches to scheduling. The steps can be done manually or a computer planning and control tool can be used.

Typical scheduling steps are:

- draw a planning network

  Take the list of activities, their durations and dependencies and produce a planning network. This provides useful information, such as what the total duration might be, given no resource constraints.

- assess resource availability

  The number of people who will be available to do the work (or the cost of buying-in resources) should now be established. The project may also require non-human resources. This availability must also be assessed.

- produce a draft schedule and assign responsibilities

  Resources are allocated to activities using the planning network plus information on resource availability. Resources are allocated in order of ascending float, i.e. allocate resources first to activities with zero float (on the critical path). Those activities with the greatest amount of spare time (float) are lowest in priority for resource allocation.

  The result will be a schedule that shows the loading of work on each person and the usage of non-people resources. The duration of each activity can be amended, based on knowledge of the resource effort required and the availability of the appropriate resource type.

- level resource usage

  The first allocation of resources may result in uneven resource usage, such as over-utilisation of some resources at certain times. This sub-process can reassign resources, move activities about within any float they may have, and change activity duration to reflect the addition or subtraction of resources. The end result of this step is a final schedule in which all activities have been assigned and which reflects the best use of available resources.

- confirm control points

  Reporting and end-of-stage activities should be added to the activity network, showing appropriate effort from the Project Manager and any support team, and a revised schedule produced.

- calculate resources and costs

  The resource requirements can now be summarised and costed to produce the plan budget.

2.7.7   Analysing Risks (PL6)

The plan should be considered a draft until the risks inherent in the plan have been identified, assessed and the plan possibly modified. All identified risks should be entered into the Risk Log.

Analysing risks and planning assumptions may result in modifications to the plan. Analysing risks runs parallel to all other planning work.

An overview of risk is given in the Management of Risk component.

Each resource should be examined for its potential risk content. Is the resource a known quantity? Are the quality of work required and the ability to meet deadlines known? Is the level of commitment known? Will the resource be totally under the control of the Project Manager? Where the answer is 'No' there is a risk involved. Countermeasures for any such risks would include tighter and more frequent monitoring until confidence in the resource is achieved. It might be better to allocate work which is either easy to do or less critical to the schedule until the skill level has been checked.

Each activity should be checked for risk. Is there any spare time or does the entire schedule depend on no slippage for the activity? Everything on the critical path, therefore, represents a risk. At the very least the countermeasures should include more frequent monitoring to give early warning of any problem. Such monitoring needs a resource and a time, so must appear in the plan (or at the very least in the Project Manager's Daily Log of things to be done).

The planning information produced so far should be examined for risks. Examples of risks that might be inherent in a plan are:

■ a sub-contractor might fail to deliver a needed product on time

■ a product delivered by a sub-contractor might be of poor quality

■ a resource may not perform at the expected level

■ a specific resource on which the plan is dependent might be removed from the project

■ external events such as a rail strike may create a crisis

■ the timetable is very tight and depends on the timely delivery of several products – any of which might be delayed.

2.7.8   Completing a Plan (PL7)

Having completed the schedule and assessment of the risks, the plan and its supporting text need to be prepared by the Project Manager for presentation to the Project Board.

The format should at least show the major products and activities that will occur throughout the plan and describe the resource requirements. The graphical presentation of the plan is normally a Gantt or bar chart. Most computerised planning and control packages provide a report in this format. Such packages also provide a report on resource requirements.

The suggested textual part of a Project Plan and a Stage Plan is given in the relevant Product Descriptions in Appendix B. Text needs to be added to explain the approach to the work, any constraints imposed, external dependencies, assumptions made, the risks identified and their recommended countermeasures. Most of the material for the narrative sections of the plan will evolve as the previous steps in the planning cycle are undertaken. Some of it will already be known because of adherence to site standards.

Tolerance margins for the plan should be agreed with the Project Board. Depending on such factors as size, complexity and risk there must be agreement on what amount of deviation from planned cost and timescale is to be allowed before the plan is considered to be out of control. Tolerances are discussed more fully in the Control component.

The products of the planning cycle should be checked for completeness and reasonableness by people experienced in planning and who know the project subject prior to presenting them formally to the Project Board for approval. Project Board approval will 'freeze' the plan as a baseline.

The Product Checklist should now have the planned start and end dates added from the final plan.

2.8   Directing a Project (DP)

This process covers the work of the Project Board at various times of the project. The concept of 'management by exception' means that we will involve the Project Board as little as possible, commensurate with the board making the key decisions. The five sub-processes here cover those key decisions.

Basically the Project Board controls the start of the project, commits resources to the project in controlled amounts (stages) and decides when the project closes.

2.8.1   Aim

The aim of the Project Board is to safeguard the interests of the customer, user and supplier throughout the project. Day-to-day management is left to the Project Manager, but the Project Board must exercise overall control and take the key decisions, such as:

- authorisation of the initiation of the project
- authorisation of the project
- liaison with corporate or programme management
- advice to the Project Manager on external events that might impact the project
- approval of Stage Plans
- ad hoc advice and direction throughout the project
- approval of stage closure
- confirmation of project closure.

Corporate or programme management

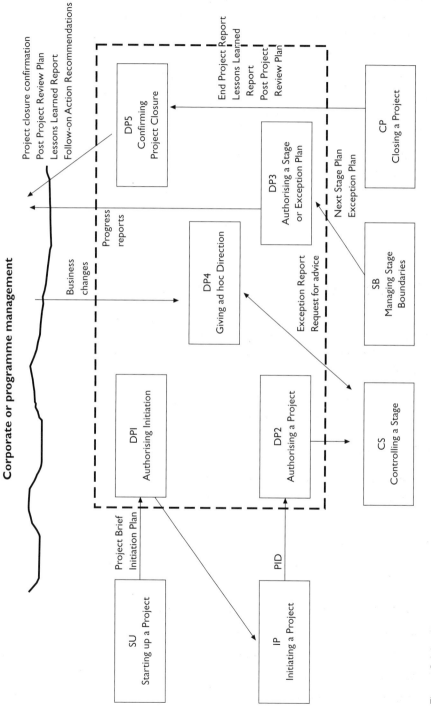

Figure 2.14

2.8.2   Authorising Initiation (DP1)

This sub-process covers the first 'formal' meeting of the Project Board. The meeting marks the official start to a project. It comes at the end of Starting Up a Project (SU) and its task is to confirm that the products of that process exist in a satisfactory form and decide if there is sufficient justification to authorise the project initiation stage. Summarised, the aims of the sub-process are to:

- check that an adequate Project Brief exists
- check and approve the Initiation Stage Plan
- agree tolerance margins for the plan
- agree control and reporting arrangements for the initiation stage
- commit the resources required to carry out the initiation stage work.

2.8.3   Authorising a Project (DP2)

In summary, this sub-process covers the Project Board work to decide whether to proceed with the project or not and, if so, whether to approve the next Stage Plan.

The initiation stage confirms that a viable project exists and that everybody concerned agrees what is to be done. Like all project work, the effort to do this needs the approval of the Project Board. The sub-process allows the Project Board to check the following before major resource commitment:

- Is everybody agreed on who is involved?
- Does everyone understand their own and everyone else's role?
- Do we agree that the project's objectives and scope are clearly defined and understood by all?
- Does a reasonable Business Case for the project exist which is adequate, clear and, wherever possible, measurable?
- Have we got the limits of our authority defined?
- Are the project's objectives in line with corporate or programme strategies and objectives?
- Can we confirm the existence of a credible Project Plan that is within the project constraints?
- Is the plan for the next stage reasonable and does it match that portion of the Project Plan?
- Are the project's estimated duration and cost within acceptable limits?
- Are the risks facing the project acceptable?

- Are adequate controls in place?
- Are tolerance levels for the project and the next stage defined?

The Project Board should expect to be consulted frequently as part of the initiation stage's work, and therefore should check on and advise the Project Manager of its own availability during the stage.

2.8.4   Authorising a Stage or Exception Plan (DP3)

This sub-process covers the work of the Project Board to authorise each stage (except initiation) and any Exception Plans that may be needed.

An important control for the Project Board is to approve only one stage at a time. At the end of one stage the Project Manager has to justify progress so far plus the plan for the next stage before being allowed to continue. Activities of the sub-process are:

- assess the results of the current stage against the approved Stage Plan plus any changes that were approved during the stage
- assess progress against the Project Plan
- assess the acceptability of the next Stage Plan against the Project Plan
- review any change to the Business Case
- review the risk status of the project
- obtain direction from corporate or programme management if the project is forecast to exceed tolerances or there has been a significant change to the Business Case
- set tolerances and reporting arrangements for the next stage
- give approval to move into the next stage (if satisfied).

The Project Board can stop the project for any reason, e.g. if the Business Case becomes invalid, project tolerances are going to be exceeded, product quality is unacceptable, or the risks become unacceptably high.

If the End Stage Assessment date was arranged some time ago and occurs before the actual end of the stage, the Project Board can give provisional approval to proceed based on one or more target dates being met to complete the current stage. If the stage finishes before the assessment, interim approval can be given to do some of the next stage work before formal approval is given. In such a case, the Project Board would clarify what work was to be done before the assessment, rather than give carte blanche to the Project Manager.

2.8.5   Giving Ad Hoc Direction (DP4)

This sub-process covers the Project Board activities when there may be a need for Project Board advice or direction outside End Stage Assessments. Its major activities are:

- advise the Project Manager about any external events that will impact the project

- give advice or direction to the Project Manager when asked

- make decisions on the action to take on receipt of an Exception Report

- monitor external events, such as business changes, which might affect the project's Business Case or risk exposure

- monitor any allocated risk situations

- keep corporate or programme management advised of project progress

- make decisions on Project Issues brought to the attention of the Project Board.

The key activity in this sub-process is deciding what action should be taken on Project Issues. The procedure to be followed should have been agreed and documented in the Project Initiation Document.

The intention of this sub-process is not to encourage general interference with the work of the Project Manager. The need for Project Board direction will be triggered by either a request for advice from the Project Manager, a problem reported in a Highlight Report or an Exception Report, or an external event that it is monitoring on behalf of the project.

2.8.6   Confirming Project Closure (DP5)

The objective of this sub-process (under normal circumstances) is to confirm that everything has been delivered, that the customer is happy and that the project can be closed. If the Project Board has decided to bring the project to a premature end, it becomes a matter of ensuring that any loose ends have been tied up and anything worthwhile saved.

The more detailed objectives of this sub-process are to:

- ensure that the project has come to a clearly defined end with an agreed handover of responsibility to the group(s) who will use, support and sustain the products

- confirm formal acceptance from the customer that the acceptance criteria set down at the outset have been met

- direct any changes which have not been implemented to an appropriate group for subsequent attention

- confirm the existence of a plan to check whether the project has produced a product that will yield the expected benefits

- recommend closure of the project to corporate or programme management.

To achieve these objectives, various steps need to be undertaken:

- ensure that all the completed products have been approved by the customer or are covered by approved concessions (if there have been any concessions, these may also be covered in Follow-on Action Recommendations).

- check that there has been a satisfactory handover of the finished product(s) to those responsible for its use and support.

- approve the Follow-on Action Recommendations and pass them to the appropriate group.

    These recommendations will have listed all the follow-on actions from the project, those Project Issues that were held back by the Project Board and any other proposals for new work stemming from the project. They may be given to the support team to implement or they may go to a programme board or strategy group for consideration as projects in their own right.

- approve the Lessons Learned Report and pass it to the appropriate body.

    A number of lessons may have been learned during the project about weaknesses or strengths of the processes, procedures, techniques and tools used, when they were used, how they were used and by whom. If there is anything which could benefit other projects within the remit of the corporate body, the Project Board has the responsibility of ensuring that this information is passed on to the relevant people, such as quality assurance.

- confirm project closure notification.

    The Project Board advises those who have provided support and resources for the project that these can now be withdrawn.

- publish and distribute the plans for the Post Project Review

- approve the End Project Report

- disband the Project Management Team.

3 BUSINESS CASE

The Business Case is a definition of the reasons for the project and the justification for undertaking the project, based on the estimated costs of the project and the expected business benefits and savings to come from use of the project's final outcome.

PRINCE2's key philosophy is that a project is driven by its Business Case. The Business Case is developed at the beginning of a project and maintained throughout the life of the project, being reviewed by the Project Board at key decision points, such as End Stage Assessments. If a satisfactory Business Case does not exist, a project should not be started. If there is a valid Business Case at the start of a project, but this justification disappears during the project, the project should be stopped. The Business Case is the most important set of information for the project. It drives the decision-making processes and is used to continually align the project's progress to the business objectives that are defined within the Business Case.

The Business Case covers the entire scope of change to the business that is affected by the project. Some Business Cases will require significant effort in their development and approval because the project will have a major impact on the organisation. Others will require less effort and involvement as the project is self-contained or has minimal impact on other parts of the organisation. Also the level of investment required will influence the rigour with which the Business Case is developed.

3.1 Business Case contents

Typical contents might include information on risks, the preferred Project Approach, a Project Plan, user requirements and so on. In PRINCE2 many of these aspects appear in other parts of the Project Initiation Document and are therefore not repeated in the PRINCE2 Business Case. As a minimum in PRINCE2, the Business Case should contain information under the following headings. These are the ones that appear under 'Composition' in the Business Case Product Description Appendix B.

3.1.1 Reasons

This section provides an explanation of the reasons why the project outcome is needed. This information should be in the Project Mandate. If not, they should be discovered and put in the Project Brief.

3.1.2 Options

This section should describe in outline the various options that were considered to achieve the desired outcome. The chosen option should be indicated, together with a summary of the reasons. This information provides assurance that alternatives were considered.

3.1.3   Benefits

This section should identify each benefit and saving that is claimed would be achieved by use of the project's outcome. Each one should be described clearly in measurable terms. It is important to define the current status of each benefit in quantifiable terms so that measurable improvements can be assessed after the project has been completed. Consideration should be given to defining how and when the measurement of improvement can be made. The Executive has the responsibility for defining benefits and savings.

A 'negative' way of assessing benefits may be useful as part of the overall justification for the project. This describes what will happen if the project is not done, e.g. the loss of market share, large maintenance costs, heavy legal penalties for non-compliance with new laws.

3.1.4   Cost and timescale

This information comes from the Project Plan. If the Project Plan is not yet completed, it may be necessary to estimate the project's costs and timescales, say from an earlier feasibility study, and refine them when the Project Plan is completed.

3.1.5   Investment appraisal

This illustrates the balance of the development, maintenance and support costs against the financial value of the benefits and savings over a period of time. This period may be a fixed number of years or the useful life of the product.

The baseline for investment appraisal is the 'do nothing' option, i.e. what the costs and benefits will be if the project is not undertaken. This is compared to the picture expected from implementing the project.

Wherever possible, benefits should be expressed in tangible ways. To start with, the Executive may define many benefits as intangible, e.g. 'happier staff'. It is worth making the effort to think carefully about intangible benefits to see if they can be expressed in more tangible ways. For example, 'happier staff' may translate into less staff turnover and/or less time off for stress-related problems. Both of these can be converted into a likely monetary saving.

There are many ways to evaluate the claimed benefits and investment appraisal. Two worth mentioning are sensitivity analysis and GAP analysis.

3.1.5.1   Sensitivity analysis

The aim is to see if the Business Case is heavily dependent on a particular benefit. If it is, this may affect project planning, monitoring and control activities and risk management, as steps would need to be taken to protect that benefit.

3.1.5.2   GAP analysis

GAP here stands for good, average and poor. It is sometimes known as best, worst and most likely cases. It consists of taking these three views of the achievement of the benefits, i.e. what are we really expecting, what might we achieve if things went well, what might be the worst-case scenario? The latter might be affected by building into the costs an allowance for estimating inaccuracies, tolerances and risks. This usually reveals if benefit expectations are reasonable or are really over-optimistic. The result of this analysis can lead to revision of the decision to go ahead with the project. This analysis would form a basis for setting tolerances.

3.2   Developing and maintaining the Business Case

The Executive is the 'owner' of the project's Business Case. It is the Executive's responsibility to ensure the project's objectives, costs, benefits, etc are correctly aligned with the business strategy or programme objectives.

The Executive may delegate the development of the Business Case to the Project Manager. However, the data upon which the case will be developed will be largely provided by the business, and responsibility for an accurate and effective Business Case remains with the Executive. On large projects, the Business Case may require a small team of experts to develop the contents. On small projects, the Business Case may only require one person to develop the information.

The Project Mandate should contain some basic elements at least of the Business Case. At this point there may be only some reasons why a solution is being sought. If the project is part of a programme, it may be just a pointer to the programme's Business Case. If the project were preceded by a feasibility study or something similar, the Project Mandate would contain a copy of the Business Case for the preferred option. Depending on how much information there was in the Project Mandate's Business Case, Starting Up a Project (SU) might be required to bring it up to a basic level in the Project Brief, containing sufficient justification for the Project Board's Authorising Initiation (DP1).

Initiating a Project (IP) is the process that fully develops the Business Case as part of the Project Initiation Document. It now contains the latest information on the costs and time to develop the product, taken from the Project Plan. If not done before, this is also where all benefits and savings will be defined (or revised) and, wherever possible, put into measurable terms. This is needed for the Project Board's Authorising a Project (DP2) and also in readiness for the post-project review.

As part of Managing Stage Boundaries (SB) the Business Case is revised for each End Stage Report with information from the stage that is closing and the next stage's plan. This revision is a major input to the Project Board in its decision in Authorising a Stage or Exception Plan (DP3).

As part of Examining Project Issues (CS4) each Project Issue is reviewed for any impact that it might have on the Business Case.

The project's Business Case provides all stakeholders with basic information about the project. The Communication Plan for the project should cover how and when the Business Case information is to be communicated to stakeholders and how they can provide feedback and raise issues concerning the Business Case.

At project closure, the Business Case is used to confirm that the project has delivered the required outcome and that the benefits expected can be realised in an appropriate timeframe by the business. The Business Case provides the basis for the Post-Project Review Plan, to ensure that the later assessment of whether the end product was successful or not is firmly linked to the Business Case.

4   ORGANISATION

In order to:

- get decisions made at the right time, by the right people
- avoid unnecessary conflict
- be able to delegate work or escalate problems

everyone involved in a project needs to know who else is involved and who has what responsibilities.

A project organisation structure identifies responsibilities, defines communication paths and reveals delegation opportunities.

PRINCE2 has a very comprehensive approach to the roles and responsibilities that are needed for a project. This does not mean that it is over-bureaucratic for smaller projects.

The PRINCE2 philosophy is to describe roles and a line of authority. These are tailored for each project. A role may be given to one individual, split between several people or combined with another role.

This chapter looks first at the project organisation structure laid down by PRINCE2 and then discusses how this might be tailored for different sizes and types of project.

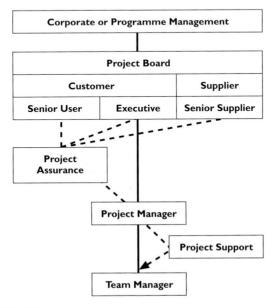

Figure 4.1 The PRINCE2 Organisation

4.1   The PRINCE2 project organisation structure

Appendix A contains a full description of the standard role descriptions. The following sections summarise those roles.

4.1.1   Project Board

The first level of delegation in a PRINCE2 project is that corporate or programme management delegates authority and responsibility for the project to a Project Board. The Project Board represents senior management's control over the project. The representations need to cover:

- the business
- the user(s) of the project's end product
- the supplier of the solution.

The roles here are normally part-time, added on to the selected senior managers' normal jobs. Because we are adding Project Board work to an already full work schedule, the aim is to keep the amount of time demanded to the minimum, commensurate with maintaining adequate control over the project. This philosophy is called Management by Exception.

Project Board members must be people who have the authority relevant for the size and criticality of the project to make 'go/no go' decisions on behalf of the project and commit the resources when a plan is approved. The limits of their authority should be established when they are appointed at the beginning of the project.

The principal responsibilities of the Project Board are:

- approval of the Project Plan and all Stage Plans
- commitment of resources to meet those plans
- definition of the limits to the Project Manager's authority
- decision on any project matters outside the Project Manager's authority
- representation of the project to the outside world.

There are three roles in the Project Board, described briefly below.

4.1.2   Executive

Some companies prefer the name 'Sponsor' or 'Senior Responsible Owner' to 'Executive'. This role is for whoever has the budget for the project, whoever is chiefly concerned with the Business Case. The main tasks of the Executive are to lead the Project Board and ensure that the project gives value for money.

The Executive is ultimately accountable for the project to corporate or programme management.

4.1.3   Senior User

The Senior User is responsible for ensuring that:

- the required product is correctly and fully specified
- the product, as it is developed, stays in line with user requirements
- any user resources required by plans approved by the Project Board are committed.

4.1.4   Senior Supplier

The Senior Supplier represents those who are charged with developing the project solution. The main responsibilities are to:

- ensure that a solution is designed and developed which will meet the specified requirements
- commit sufficient supplier resources to meet the needs of plans approved by the Project Board
- be responsible for the supplier's Business Case if this is different to the customer's Business Case.

4.1.5   Project Manager

The Project Board gives the Project Manager authority to run one stage of the project at a time on a day-to-day basis on its behalf within constraints which are laid down at the time of approving that plan. At the end of each stage the Project Manager must show the Project Board:

- the results of that stage
- the plan for the next stage
- the current status of the Business Case, the risks and the Project Plan

and request approval to move into the next stage. This is a major control point for the Project Board.

The Project Manager's prime responsibility is to ensure that the project produces the required products to the required standard of quality within the specified time and budget. As a project is driven by its Business Case, the Project Manager must produce a result that is capable of achieving the benefits defined in the Business Case.

4.1.6   Team Manager

The use of this role is optional. The Project Manager may find it easier to delegate the authority and responsibility for planning the creation of certain products and managing a team to produce those products. This is most likely when a supplier or sub-contractor is used to develop some products. Other reasons for using the Team Manager role are geographic location or the need for specialist skills outside the Project Manager's experience.

The Team Manager role agrees a workload with the Project Manager on behalf of the team, plans and controls the performance of that work, reports progress to the Project Manager, and is responsible for obtaining the necessary approval of the resulting products.

4.1.7   Project Assurance

There is a need for each member of the Project Board to feel that he or she has available an independent assessment of progress, plans, risks, Business Case impacts and quality – independent, that is, of the Project Manager.

Each member of the Project Board decides how that assurance is to be carried out, whether it will carry out its own assurance or delegate some or all of the assurance role to others.

Project Assurance cannot be delegated to the Project Manager, because that would not be an independent view.

4.1.8   Project Support

Again this role is optional. The Project Manager may need administrative help, either because of the sheer volume of administrative work or because of insufficient expertise in the use of required project management tools. Examples of the latter are planning and control software packages and configuration management tools.

The Project Manager directs Project Support staff.

4.2   Practical tips

For a very small internal project, the Sponsor might take all three of the Project Board roles. For small projects it may be possible to combine the roles of Executive and Senior User.

Where the final product will affect several departments, it may be necessary to share the Senior User role between them. Pragmatically, there should be an upper limit on how many people share the role, otherwise Project Board meetings can take too long. Another problem can be that they outnumber and overwhelm the other members of the Project Board. A sensible maximum would be three people sharing the Senior User role.

In cases where many people wish to share the Senior User role, a good device is to form them all into a User Committee. The committee appoints a chairman. This person canvasses the opinions of the committee before Project Board meetings, represents the committee at the meetings and reports back to the committee on the outcome of the meetings. Members of a User Committee can receive any project information they desire. These needs are documented in the Communication Plan, described in Chapter 5 which deals with control.

Where an outside supplier is being used, some people get nervous about giving a supplier representative a seat on the Project Board. An alternative is to use the customer's Contracts Manager. This person would then have to assure the other Project Board members that the necessary supplier resources could be obtained. Assuring other members of the Project Board of the quality of delivered products in such a case would probably require this area of Project Assurance to be delegated.

In a small- or medium-sized project the Project Manager often incorporates the Team Manager's job with his or her own role.

In small projects the Project Manager often carries out the Project Support duties.

5   CONTROL

5.1   Overview

Control has three elements: monitoring, detecting deviations and taking corrective actions. This applies to both the management and technical activities of PRINCE.

Figure 5.1 shows a graphic overview of PRINCE controls.

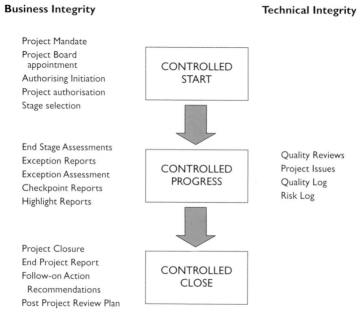

Business Integrity   **Technical Integrity**

Project Mandate
Project Board
   appointment   CONTROLLED
Authorising Initiation   START
Project authorisation
Stage selection

End Stage Assessments   Quality Reviews
Exception Reports   CONTROLLED   Project Issues
Exception Assessment   PROGRESS   Quality Log
Checkpoint Reports   Risk Log
Highlight Reports

Project Closure
End Project Report   CONTROLLED
Follow-on Action   CLOSE
   Recommendations
Post Project Review Plan

Figure 5.1

5.2   Business integrity

The business integrity of a project covers keeping it on schedule and within cost estimates. Monitoring it means comparing actual effort and cost against what was planned, plus reporting on the findings. If evidence shows that the actuals will move outside the tolerance levels agreed for the plan in the near future this would trigger corrective action by the Project Manager or escalation of the problem to the Project Board.

The major management controls come at the beginning of the project (Project start-up and initiation), at the end of the project (Project Closure) and at the end of each stage (End Stage Assessment). If the situation described in the last paragraph occurs, the meeting with the Project Board would be an exception assessment. These are all face-to-face meetings. In between these a regular Highlight Report sent from the Project Manager allows the Project Board to monitor the project in their care. Information to update the plans comes from frequent checkpoint meetings of the project team.

5.3   Technical integrity

Does the product meet its specification? This includes functionality, performance, reliability and maintainability. The product is checked against its specification, the Product Description and the acceptance criteria. Monitoring is done by such checks as quality review and testing. There are also Checklists in Appendix D to assist in monitoring the quality. Detection of deviations will trigger either a quality follow-up action or a Project Issue, leading to correction of the situation.

Another technical control in PRINCE is Configuration Management. This is discussed in Chapter 9.

5.4   Management controls

5.4.1   Stages

5.4.1.1   What is a stage?

Stages are divisions of a project with a decision point at their end. A stage is a collection of activities and products whose delivery is managed as a unit. As such it is a subset of the project, and in PRINCE2 terms it is the element of work which the Project Manager is managing on behalf of the Project Board at any one time. The use of stages in a PRINCE2 project is mandatory. The number of stages is flexible and depends on the needs of the project.

5.4.1.2   Why are stages important?

The division of a project into stages is an important control for the Project Board. The Project Board's commitment is limited to only the current stage. At the end of each stage it can get an update on the status of the Project Plan, the Business Case and risks as well as a view of the next Stage Plan before deciding whether to commit to the next stage.

The breakdown of a project into stages allows the Project Board 'management by exception'. It gives the Project Manager authority to get on with a stage. By setting tolerance levels the Project Board ensures that it will get warning of any potential deviation beyond these tolerances and a chance to redirect the project without the need for regular progress meetings.

The concept of stages is important to the Project Manager in that it allows detailed planning of only as much of the project as can be done with confidence, and reduces the planning work at the beginning of a project. Each stage of the project is only planned in detail immediately before that part of the project is about to start, thus allowing the Project Manager to gain as much information about it as possible from the work which has gone on before.

There should always be an initiation stage in a PRINCE2 project. The initiation stage is essential to ensure that there is a firm basis for the project, understood by all parties. Every project should therefore consist of at least two stages. A small project may need only two stages: an initiation stage and the remainder of the project as the second stage.

The main reasons for breaking a project into stages are summarised below.

5.4.1.3   Review and decision points

Where a risky project lasts for more than a few weeks there may be a need to limit commitment to only the current part of the project, at which time the Project Board can review the continuing viability of the project and make decisions on further commitments.

PRINCE2 uses stages to deal with these decision points. The decisions and the information on which they are based form the basis of the End Stage Assessments. The benefits these End Stage Assessments bring to the project are:

- encouraging the Project Board to reassess the project viability at regular intervals, rather than let it run on in an uncontrolled manner

- ensuring that key decisions are made prior to the detailed work needed to implement them

- providing minimal 'intervention' by the Project Board to retain its overall control of a project which is performing within the tolerances laid down.

5.4.1.4   Planning horizons

Uncertainty can often mean that it is only possible to plan in detail the activities and products of a limited amount of the work of the project. The rest of the project's work can only be planned in broad outline. The adoption of stages handles this situation by having two different but related levels of plan, i.e. a detailed Stage Plan and an outline Project Plan.

5.4.1.5   Scale

Most projects need to be broken down into more manageable stages to enable the correct level of planning and control to be exercised.

5.4.1.6   How to define stages

The process of defining stages is fundamentally a process of balancing:

- how far ahead the Project Board is prepared to commit funds and resources

- how far ahead in a project it is sensible for the Project Manager to try to plan in detail
- where the key decision points need to be on a risky project
- having too many small stages versus too few big ones (avoiding too many End Stage Assessments).

This will be a balance of the factors identified above, and will be influenced by any Team Plans. However, the Project Manager will have to reconcile the Stage Plan and any associated Team Plans.

5.4.1.7   How to use stages

There are several factors to consider when choosing the number of stages for a project:

- the exposure of the project to risks (and any key moments when these may occur)
- the duration of the project
- the products whose development will cause a large outlay of resources
- the uncertainty about some future aspect of the work.

The PRINCE2 technique of product-based planning is invaluable here since by using it the Project Manager can identify all the products which are due to be produced in any given stage. This can then be used to assess completion or otherwise of the stage.

5.4.2   Project Mandate

Management triggers off a project by giving the Project Manager instructions on what they want done. This, then, is their first control. Since this instruction is created before PRINCE2 begins, the Project Manager has little or no control over its format and content.

5.4.3   Authorising Initiation (DP1)

The first official meeting of the Project Board is to check that the Project Manager has got sufficient information to create the Project Initiation Document, the 'contract' between the Project Board and the Project Manager for the project work, and a plan for the production of the Project Initiation Document. This meeting can be as formal or informal as the specific project needs.

5.4.4   Authorising a Project (DP2)

The next meeting of the Project Board (in normal circumstances) is at the end of the initiation stage, when it is asked to approve the Project Initiation Document. Again, this meeting can be formal or informal.

5.4.4.1   Objectives

The objectives of the Project Board at this meeting should be:

- to formally initiate the project
- to ensure that
  - ☐ the project starts on a firm business footing
  - ☐ the project objectives are clear
  - ☐ all concerned understand their responsibilities and have the appropriate level of authority
- to approve the Project Plan and next Stage Plan
- to commit resources to the next stage.

All this is documented in the Project Initiation Document. If the entire document cannot be approved at the first meeting, as many decisions as possible should be taken, and those parts of the next Stage Plan approved where reasonable. Note should be made of work to complete or update the document and responsibilities allocated. The format of that meeting is an End Stage Assessment.

5.4.5   End Stage Assessment (DP3)

The End Stage Assessment (ESA) is a mandatory control at the end of each stage. Its formality will depend on the project situation.

5.4.5.1   Attendees

- Project Board
- Project Manager
- Project Assurance (if applicable).

5.4.5.2   Objectives

- To review the performance of the stage which has just finished against budget and schedule
- To review the status and quality of the stage products
- To present the plans for the next stage
- To review the Project Plans in the light of the last stage and the plans for the next stage
- To ensure that the project is still viable (i.e. review an update of the project Business Case and risk situation)
- To set the tolerance level for the next Stage Plan

■ To give authority to proceed to the next stage.

5.4.5.3   Agenda

■ The Project Manager presents a summary of the current stage

■ Those with Project Assurance responsibilities present a review of:

☐ user satisfaction with products delivered so far

☐ quality-checking work carried out

☐ the status of Project Issues

☐ the use of standards and their effectiveness.

■ The Project Manager and Project Board discuss any change requests received and their planned actions

■ The Project Manager presents the next Stage Plan

■ The impact of the next Stage Plan is reviewed against the Project Plan

■ The updated Project Plan is reviewed by the Project Manager against the Business Case

■ Those with assurance responsibilities present their assessments of the next Stage Plan

■ The Project Board makes a decision on whether to approve the Stage Plan.

5.4.6   Exception Report

Where the Project Manager forecasts that tolerance levels for the stage or the project are going to be exceeded, the situation must be reported to the Project Board for its decision on what action to take. The Project Manager submits an Exception Report that details:

■ the situation which will cause the deviation

■ the options available

■ the impact of these on the Business Case, risks and Project Plan

■ the Project Manager's recommendation.

In response (see process DP4) the Project Board may revise the tolerance levels to remove the problem, decide that the project is no longer viable and should be closed, or ask the Project Manager to submit an Exception Plan.

If the user decides that one or more Requests For Change must be implemented and the Project Manager says that they cannot be done within the present plan, this is a situation which would cause an Exception Report.

5.4.7   Exception Assessment (DP3)

An exception assessment is held to consider an Exception Plan, requested by the Project Board following its consideration (DP4) of a forecast deviation from plan which would cause the agreed tolerance levels to be exceeded. Its formality depends on the specific project situation.

5.4.7.1   Attendees

- Project Board
- Project Manager
- Project Assurance.

5.4.7.2   Objectives

The objectives of the Exception Assessment are:

- to review progress of the current stage against its plans
- to ensure that the project is still viable
- to review and approve the Exception Plan
- to review the tolerance levels for the Exception Plan
- to authorise the project to continue.

5.4.8   Checkpoint meetings

5.4.8.1   Attendees

- Team Leader (or Project Manager if Team Manager role not used)
- Team members
- Project Assurance (optional).

5.4.8.2   Objectives

The objectives of checkpoint meetings are:

- to review progress against individual Work Packages
- to discuss solutions to team problems
- to identify targets for the next checkpoint period
- to circulate departmental and project information.

Checkpoint meetings are held on a regular basis, usually weekly.

5.4.9   Highlight Report

5.4.9.1   Circulation

The Highlight Report should be circulated from the Project Manager to:

- Project Board
- Project Assurance
- any other stakeholders mentioned in the Communication Plan.

5.4.9.2   Objectives

The objectives of the Highlight Report are:

- to provide a periodic summary of the stage progress to the Project Board and stakeholders
- to highlight any real or potential problems
- to forecast progress over the next period.

The Project Board decides on the frequency of the Highlight Reports at the outset of the project and this is recorded in the Project Initiation Document. This depends on the size, importance and risk of the project, but should not be less frequent than monthly.

Its production is the responsibility of the Project Manager. It is prepared from the accumulated Checkpoint Reports. One side of paper should be the target. The format of the report is shown in Appendix B and a sample is given in Appendix F.

5.4.10   Communication Plan

One entry in the Project Initiation Document will be the Communication Plan. It plays an important part in control by identifying who needs to receive information from the project and who needs to provide information to the project. A suggested description of its contents is given in the Product Description outlines, Appendix B. Briefly, it shows:

- who needs information
- what information they need
- when they need it
- the format in which it should be presented.

It should include senior or programme management, stakeholders and other interested parties, such as those who will have to support the product in its operational life.

5.4.11   Confirming Project Closure (DP5)

5.4.11.1   Attendees

- Project Board
- Project Manager
- Project Assurance
- Management representing other interests, such as support and maintenance of the finished product may also be invited.

5.4.11.2   Objectives

The objectives of Project Closure are:

- to close the project in an orderly and structured manner
- to confirm that all products have been completed
- to confirm that all Project Issues and Quality Review Action Lists have been closed
- to confirm that all documentation necessary to operate and maintain the end product is available, referenced and filed
- to confirm that the customer and those responsible for its future support accept the finished product
- to confirm the existence of a plan to investigate achievement of the expected benefits by the delivered product (Post Project Review plan)
- to pass on to an appropriate body any useful lessons learned during the project (Lessons Learned Report)
- to record whether the project was a success when measured against its Project Initiation Document (End Project Report).

The Project Closure is usually combined with the final End Stage Assessment.

5.4.11.3   Agenda

Items on the agenda should include:

- review the End Project Report
- ensure that all products are complete and delivered
- ensure that all files are complete and archived
- ensure that the customer and product support accept the end product(s)
- confirm that all Project Issues have been closed

- confirm that any unactioned Project Issues have been submitted as Follow-on Action Recommendations to the product's maintenance and support group
- if there is a central quality assurance function, ensure that the quality file has been handed to them
- ensure that all training materials have been handed over to the person or group who will be responsible
- confirm that a general plan has been made of how and when the product can be checked to see if it has achieved the expected business benefits
- hand over a Lessons Learned Report for transfer by the Project Board to the relevant body
- make a final report to the corporate or programme management that appointed the Project Board.

5.5   Technical controls

5.5.1   Quality reviews

A quality review is a structured review of a document by a group of people in a planned, documented and organised fashion. The primary purpose of a quality review is to check the quality of a product. But it also enhances the status information about the Stage Plan. It is one thing to be told by a team member that a product is complete, but much greater confidence is felt if it is confirmed by a quality review that the product is error-free.

5.5.2   Project Issues

5.5.2.1   Introduction

A Project Issue is used by anyone to raise issues relating to the project. The subject of a Project Issue is limited only in so far as it must in some way relate to the project. It may address a technical problem, for example:

- a perceived error in the product
- a failure of the product to meet user requirements
- an inconsistency between one version of a product and any of its earlier versions.

It may be triggered by a need by the user to change the specification, such as:

- an idea for an improvement in design, functionality, user interface, documentation, standards etc.
- a forgotten function
- a change in policy or legislation.

Alternatively, it may address a management issue, perhaps related to budgets, plans, schedules, projected staff or skill shortages.

There are three types of Project Issue within the PRINCE2 methodology. These are used to document desired change to, or some failure in, a product or the project. They are:

- Off-Specification (OS)
- Request For Change (RFC)
- any question or concern not covered by the two types listed above.

The configuration librarian logs all Project Issues. If this role has not been allocated, control of issues will be the responsibility of the appropriate Project or Team Manager.

Project Issues can be raised at any point during the project.

A Project Issue is submitted first to the configuration librarian, who enters it in the Issue Log and allocates a unique identifier.

A copy of the Project Issue is sent to the author. The issue should then be assessed for its impact. The technical impact covers:

- which products would have to be changed
- how much effort this would take
- what the impact would be on the plan (including the Project Plan)
- the cost of the proposed change.

The business impact would cover:

- the effect on the Business Case
- the effect on the risks.

There should be a regular examination of all open Project Issues. The frequency of this depends on how many reports are being received and how close they are to the end of the stage. It is the responsibility of the Project Manager to decide what action to take on a Project Issue.

When a Project Issue is closed it is the responsibility of the configuration librarian to inform the originator of what action was taken.

By the end of the project all Project Issues must have been closed, either by rejection, action or transfer to the Follow-on Action Recommendations.

5.5.2.2   Errors discovered at a quality review

Errors discovered at a quality review are not normally put on a Project Issue. This would only happen if the error relates to a different product than the one being reviewed, or the error is one which cannot easily be corrected via the normal follow-up procedures.

5.5.2.3   Off-Specification

An Off-Specification is used to document any technical situation where the product is failing to meet its specification. Because the error(s) it describes might not be corrected before the product goes live, Off-Specifications are filed with the relevant Product Description.

Off-Specifications are confirmed by the Project Manager. When an Off-Specification is raised, it should be accompanied by supporting evidence and in such detail that someone else can recreate the problem.

The more experienced team members are usually given the job of technical evaluation of work required to correct the Off-Specification and its priority. An allowance should be made in a Stage Plan for an appropriate amount of their time to do these assessments. The configuration librarian assists the impact analysis by identifying from the configuration records what other products would be affected by the failure. The person or persons charged with business assurance would normally assess the business impact. On receiving the assessed Off-Specification the Project Manager has one of four normal options:

- the work can be done within the current Stage Plan limits
- the work can be delayed without detriment to the project until the next Stage Plan where it can be put in as a normal activity
- the work cannot be done within the tolerance bounds of the Stage Plan and an Exception Report must be raised and presented to the Project Board
- if the corrective work affects other products which have already been approved by the Project Board, the Project Manager must ask for the board's approval in an Exception Report to amend the products in question.

Any change in the status of an Off-Specification must be notified to the configuration librarian so that the file copy can be kept up to date and the originator notified. On receipt of a completed Off-Specification the librarian should ensure that all affected products have been resubmitted to the library.

5.5.2.4   Request For Change

A Request For Change records a proposed modification to the product.

When the configuration librarian has logged the Request For Change in the Issue Log, it is passed for impact analysis, helped by the configuration librarian, to identify what products are affected. Having assessed the resource effort needed, the request is costed. The Requests For Change are then given by the Project Manager to the Project Board. The Project Board has the task of sorting the requests into priority order and making decisions on what action to take.

The Project Board makes its decision:

- to cancel the request
- to defer it to a later enhancement project
- to have it implemented by the current project.

In the last case the Project Manager decides whether the approved change(s) can or cannot be implemented within the current Stage Plan. If the effort and/or cost would take the stage outside the tolerance margins, it requires the submission of an Exception Report to the Project Board.

Figure 5.2 shows the sequence of events in handling an issue.

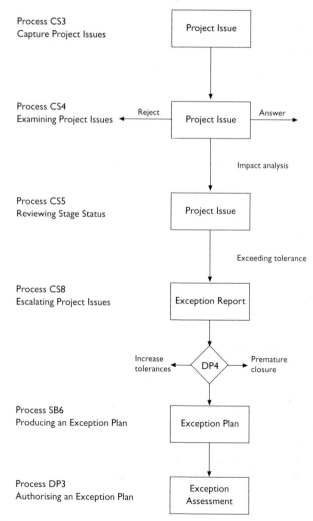

Figure 5.2

6 PLAN

6.1 Objectives of planning

A plan is a proposal to meet identified targets for products, timescales, costs and quality. In order to define this proposal, a plan must include a range of essential information and lay down a number of essential activities.

A plan must:

- define the products to be produced
- chart the activities needed to produce each product
- specify how quality will be controlled
- define resource requirements
- define timescales
- show the cost build-up
- identify and allocate responsibilities
- provide a means of establishing team and individual objectives
- facilitate control and identify control points
- facilitate project communication.

6.2 Levels of plan

As shown in Figure 6.1, there are four possible planning levels within the PRINCE framework:

- Project Plan
- Stage Plans
- Team Plans
- Exception Plan.

6.2.1 Project Plan

The Project Plan is a mandatory plan in PRINCE2. It shows the major products of the whole project and the time and resources required. This information will be shown in more detail in lower level plans. The Project Plan is prepared once for the whole project as part of the Project Initiation Document. It is a high level plan of the entire project, to give management an idea of the commitment needed.

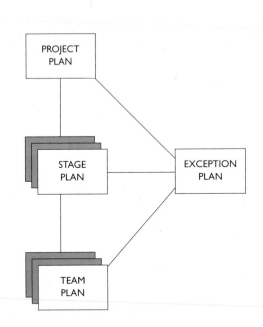

Figure 6.1

Rather than commit to the whole project at the start, the Project Board will usually ask for the project to be broken into stages. At the end of each stage the Project Board reviews the status of the whole project before deciding whether to commit to the next stage. So the end of a stage represents a major decision point for the Project Board. The division into the various stages is shown on the Project Plan.

6.2.2   Stage Plans

A stage is a part of a project which the Project Board agrees can be managed by the Project Manager without the need for further decisions from the Project Board, provided that progress stays within defined bounds, e.g. time and cost.

A Stage Plan is prepared just before the start of that stage. This is the level of plan against which the Project Manager will exercise day-to-day control, so the products or activities need to be broken down into work elements which will only take a few days (say five to ten) to complete. Stage Plans are also mandatory in PRINCE2. In a very small project of two stages (initiation and the rest of the project) it may be sufficient to include the detail of the stages in the Project Plan.

6.2.3   Team Plans

The use of Team Plans is optional. They are normally only required where a number of teams are working simultaneously on different products for the project. A Team Plan shows the work for one team and is a subset of the Stage Plan. Where Team Plans are used, they will be at a detailed level to allow the Team Managers to control the teams' work against these plans, and the Stage Plan will be a summary of the various Team Plans.

6.2.4   Exception Plan

An Exception Plan is usually required where costs or timescales have been forecast to exceed the tolerance set by the Project Board for a plan. The Project Manager by means of an Exception Report has reported the problem to the Project Board. The Project Board has a number of options in response to an Exception Report, one of which is to ask the Project Manager to raise an Exception Plan. It is created to replace the remainder of the plan that cannot now be met. It has the same structure as the plan that it replaces.

6.3   Plan Structure

The Plan Structure consists of a Graphical Summary (usually a Gantt or bar chart) and the Plan Text.

The Plan Text complements the graphical data with other information to put the graphs in perspective and provide additional information. It consists of:

- Plan Description, containing:
  - project identification
  - the plan level (project, stage or exception)
  - stage identification
  - a narrative summary of the plan and its background
  - intended implementation approach
  - constraints or objectives which have affected the plan.
- Plan Assumptions

  The bases upon which the plan has been constructed, e.g. specific resources or skill levels, user priorities, staff rates, discount factors used etc.

- External Dependencies

  If the plan depends for its success on elements which are beyond the Project Manager's control, such as deliveries by suppliers, contract agencies, data or products from other projects, these must be described.

- Plan Prerequisites

  What must be in place in order for the plan to work, e.g. programmers recruited, users assigned, training done, equipment installed and building work completed.

- Plan Risks

  Specific areas of risk which have been identified and must be closely monitored, e.g. overlapping activities, staffing concerns etc. This should include the planner's assessment of how serious and how likely is the risk. It is important to document these in the Risk Log because the Project Board may have information which suggests a different view of a risk.

- Tolerance

  This sets the limits of authority for the person managing the plan and should reflect the confidence level in the plan. Tolerance figures are normally given for time and cost. If the actuals are likely to move above or below the tolerance margins, this triggers the production of an Exception Report to the Project Board.

- Reporting

  The methods, source and destination, frequency and formats for monitoring and reporting on performance during the life of the plan should be stated as part of the plan text.

7   QUALITY

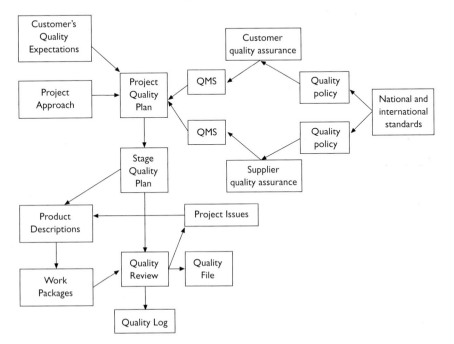

Figure 7.1 The PRINCE2 Quality Path

The path to quality in PRINCE2 is shown in Figure 7.1. Each element of the diagram will be explained with cross-references to the areas of PRINCE2 that relate to it.

7.1   Customer's quality expectations

The supplier cannot plan to provide the customer with a quality product until both customer and supplier understand and agree what that quality should be. Quality considerations begin by defining what the customer's quality expectations are. This should be done in the process Starting Up a Project (SU).

Quality expectations could be considered under a number of headings, such as:

■ functional requirements

■ performance

■ practicability

■ security

- compatibility
- reliability
- maintainability
- expandability
- flexibility
- clarity
- comparison to another product
- cost
- delivery date.

7.2   ISO 9001

ISO 9001 is part of an international standard for quality products, issued under the authority of the International Organisation for Standardisation (ISO). It applies to quality assurance in the design/development, production, installation and servicing of a product.

A company can use the quality standard ISO 9001 when:

- setting up a quality assurance function
- examining the quality assurance product of a supplier.

It therefore may have several impacts on the quality considerations for a project:

- it may have been used by the customer and/or the supplier as a checklist when creating its quality management system
- the supplier's development methods may be accredited under ISO 9001
- the customer may wish to match a supplier's quality methods against the requirements of ISO 9001 or insist on a supplier who holds ISO 9001 accreditation
- it may have been used as the basis for the corporate quality policy of the supplier.

7.3   Quality policy

The customer and/or the supplier may have a quality policy. This may be a simple statement laying down the company's attitude towards quality. If it has any meaning, it should direct and influence the supplier's attitude in construction, testing and reaction to any customer complaints about quality.

If both customer and supplier have quality policies, it is sensible to check that they are in harmony.

7.4   Quality management system

Two things should follow up a quality policy: a quality management system (QMS) and a quality organisation structure.

The QMS is a set of standards that cover all the normal work done by that company. Each standard will cover the techniques, tools, required expertise and steps to be used in the creation of a specific type of product. If the product is a document, the standard will also cover its format or appearance.

If both the customer and supplier have quality management systems, there must be agreement on which QMS or what amalgamation of standards from both sets of standards will be used.

7.5   Quality assurance

Responsibility for setting and monitoring the standards should be given to a group, normally known as quality assurance. The corporate organisation structure should indicate where responsibility for quality lies. One of the considerations when creating the project organisation structure is whether the independent quality assurance group needs representation on the project, e.g. as part of Project Assurance.

7.6   Project Approach

How the project plans to meet the customer's quality expectations will be affected by the approach chosen for the provision of the end product. Typical approaches would include:

- the product is built from scratch by the customer's staff
- an external supplier builds the product from scratch
- the product is built from scratch with contributions from many external organisations
- an existing product is modified to meet the new needs
- an off-the-shelf product is bought.

Quality checking methods and responsibilities will vary according to the chosen approach.

The Project Approach is confirmed as part of Starting Up a Project (SU), therefore it is in place and can be used by the initiation sub-process Planning Quality (IP1).

It is normally impossible to be involved in the testing of an off-the-shelf product. A privileged customer might be asked to participate in an alpha or beta test of a product, but this only happens when the organisation is already a customer. Checks on the quality of such products can be made with existing customers. Sometimes for more expensive products there is a trial period when testing can be done.

PRINCE2 offers a good method of checking quality where a product is to be developed by external contractors. This is through use of the Project Assurance function. Each time that an external team manager plans work for the project, the Project Assurance role should insist on seeing the draft plan. The purpose is to identify products being developed in the plan which are of interest to the assurance function. Project Assurance then verify that quality checking arrangements for these products are satisfactory. This covers the method of inspection, the points in the products' development when inspections are to be held and the people to be involved in the inspection. There should be the option to specify people to be included in the inspections for the purpose of Project Assurance. This is particularly relevant and important for the user's/customer's specialist assurance. *One word of warning.* This requirement to inspect and modify the contractor's plans should be included in the contract.

7.7   Project Quality Plan

This is created in the process Initiating a Project (IP). It forms part of the Project Initiation Document. It defines in general terms how the project will meet the customer's quality expectations.

It will identify the techniques and standards to be used. If there is a QMS in existence, it is normally sufficient to simply point to the QMS manual that contains the standards. If necessary, the Project Quality Plan will identify any standards in the QMS that will not be used, or any extra standards not in the QMS which will be used.

The plan should also identify quality responsibilities for the project. For example, if the customer or the supplier has a quality assurance function, this would explain how that function would play a part in the project. This links with the Organisation component of PRINCE2, where the external quality assurance function would take a Project Assurance role.

7.8   Stage Quality Plan

Encompassed within a Stage Plan will be details of how the Project Quality Plan will be implemented in that stage. This will go down to the level of each product to be produced in the stage, defining how its quality will be tested or checked and who will be involved in each check. For example, if the product is a document which is to be quality reviewed, the Stage Plan should show the time and effort allocation of the chairman and Reviewers to be used. The Stage Plan should show in diagrammatic form when the review will take place and how long it will take.

The Stage Plan is a key time for the involvement of the Project Assurance function. On production of a draft Stage Plan, the Project Manager should discuss the quality requirements with those appointed to a Project Assurance role, particularly user and specialist assurance. They have the opportunity to identify the products that are important to those whose interests they represent. They can then insist on:

■ identifying people who should be involved in the check

■ the points in the development of the product where it should be reviewed.

This is particularly important where work is being allocated to an external team. Rather than wait until the 'finished' product is handed over for acceptance trials, it is better for the final user to have people checking the product all the way through its design and development. Finding out that a product doesn't meet requirements during its acceptance trials is expensively late, maybe fatally so.

Note: Where external teams are to be used, it is important to define in the contract that Project Assurance has the right to see draft plans and insist on their people being part of quality checks wherever they wish.

7.9   Product Descriptions and quality criteria

There should be a Product Description for each major product to be created during each Stage Plan. This indicates, among other things, the quality criteria that the product must meet and the method of checking that those criteria exist in the finished product.

It is very sensible, even essential, to involve the customer's staff in defining the Product Descriptions, including the quality criteria. Not only are they the people who should know best, but if the product meets their quality criteria, it is very difficult for them to refuse to accept the product.

An inherent quality criterion for every product is that the product should satisfy the other elements of the Product Description. For example, it should contain those elements mentioned under 'Composition' and be capable of satisfying the defined purpose of the product. A general set of quality criteria is given at the start of Appendix B, Product Descriptions.

7.10   Quality review

The detailed steps of a quality review are explained in its own chapter. Basically it is a structured review of a document by a group of people in a planned, documented and organised fashion. The people involved have been planned as part of creating the Stage Plan. The technique links with the configuration management part of the project organisation, which will be responsible for releasing copies of the document to be reviewed, freezing the original copy and updating the status of the product.

There is also a link with Project Support, which might undertake the organisation of the review and the dissemination of the documentation.

7.11   Quality Log

The Quality Log is created during Initiating a Project (IP). It holds the record of all the quality checking done in the project. The Project Manager adds to the log all planned quality checking activities. The Team Manager or individual team member charged with the development and testing of a product updates the Quality Log with the dates and results of each quality check, and it then forms an audit trail of the quality work done in the project.

7.12   Project Issues

Project Issues have many potential impacts on quality. A Project Issue may be reporting a quality problem with a product. It might be thought that such problems would be handled on an action list as part of a quality review or some other test. But a quality problem may be found in a product that has already been approved, or a review might discover a problem in a product that is not the one being inspected. There is also the possibility that an action item from a quality review may be found to require a lot of time, beyond the short time frame expected for the solution of a quality review action item. It may even be decided, because of time constraints, to approve a product that contains an error. In both these cases the error can be transferred to a Project Issue, so that a record exists and the error will not be overlooked.

The other point to mention here is that if a Project Issue requires changes to one or more products, the relevant Product Descriptions should be checked to see if they also need changing.

8 THE MANAGEMENT OF RISK

8.1 Introduction

Risk can be defined as:

> 'the chance of exposure to the adverse consequences of future events'.

By their nature projects are set up to deal with change, and hence the future is less predictable than is typically the case with routine work. In addition, projects can be large and complex, and can be dealing with novel or unusual factors. Risk is therefore a major factor to be considered during the management of a project.

Part of a Project Manager's job concerns managing a project's exposure to risk (that is, the probability of identified risks occurring and the potential impact if they do occur). The aim is to keep exposure to an acceptable level in a cost-effective way.

Every project is subject to constant change in its business and wider environment. The risk environment is constantly changing too. The project's priorities and relative importance of risks will shift and change. Assumptions about risk have to be regularly revisited and reconsidered, for example at each End Stage Assessment.

In order to contain the risks during a project, they must be managed in a structured manner, otherwise the situation will lack order and be unmanageable. This structure consists of two phases:

- risk analysis, which involves the identification and evaluation of risks, plus the selection of appropriate actions
- risk management, which covers the activities involved in the planning, resourcing, monitoring and controlling of actions, which will address the threats and problems identified, so as to improve the likelihood of the project achieving its stated objectives.

8.2 Risk Log

Once identified, risks are all entered in the Risk Log. This is a summary document of all risks, their assessment, owners and status. A suggested list of contents is given in Appendix B. The Risk Log is a control tool for the Project Manager, providing a quick reference to the key risks facing the project, what monitoring activities should be taking place and by whom. Reference to it can lead to entries in the Project Manager's Daily Log to check on a risk.

8.3 Budgeting for risk management

A project needs to allocate the appropriate budget, time and resources to risk management. The risk process must be embedded in the project environment, rather than being tacked on as an afterthought. The cost of carrying out the risk process and the level of commitment and time, such as contingency plans, risk avoidance or reduction, needs to be recognised and agreed. Whilst budget may be allocated to actions relating to risk treatment, there is often a failure to provide sufficient budget to the earlier parts of the process, such as risk assessment that can require a diverse range of skills, tools and techniques. Experience has shown that allocating the correct budget to the risk process early on will pay dividends later.

8.4   Risk tolerance

Another name for this is 'risk appetite'. Before determining what to do about risks, a project must consider the amount of risk it is prepared to tolerate. This will vary according to the perceived importance of particular risks. For example, the view of financial risks, and how much the project is prepared to put at risk will depend on a number of variables, such as budgets, the effect on other parts of the programme or organisation, or additional risks such as political embarrassment. A project may be prepared to take comparatively large risks in some areas and none at all in others, such as risks to health and safety. Risk tolerance can be related to the four tolerance parameters; risk to completion within timescale and/or cost, and to achieving product quality and project scope within the boundaries of the Business Case.

Perceptions of tolerance have to be considered in detail to establish the optimum balance of a risk occurring against the costs and value for money of limiting that risk. The organisation's overall tolerance of exposure to risk must also be considered as well as a view of individual risks.

8.5   Risk responsibilities

The management of risk is one of the most important parts of the job done by the Project Board and the Project Manager. The Project Manager is responsible for ensuring that risks are identified, recorded and regularly reviewed. The Project Board has four responsibilities:

- notifying the Project Manager of any external risk exposure to the project
- making decisions on the Project Manager's recommended reactions to risk
- striking a balance between level of risk and the potential benefits that the project may achieve
- notifying corporate or programme management of any risks that affect the project's ability to meet corporate or programme constraints.

The Project Manager modifies plans to include agreed actions to avoid or reduce the impact of risks.

Risk analysis requires input from the management of the organisation. The organisation's management, in turn, is kept informed by the Project Board of the risk analysis results.

Communication is particularly important between the project and programme levels within the organisation. Where the project is part of a programme, the management of risk procedures used by the project must be consistent and compatible with those of the programme unless there are valid reasons not to do so. Where a risk is uncovered in the programme, any affected projects should be involved in the analysis of that risk. Similarly, project risk evaluation should include staff from the programme. Project risks that threaten programme milestones or objectives must be escalated to programme management.

8.5.1   Risk ownership

An 'owner' should be identified for each risk, who should be the person best situated to keep an eye on it. The Project Manager will normally suggest the 'owner' and the Project Board make the decision. Project Board members may be appointed 'owners' of risks, particularly risks from sources external to the project.

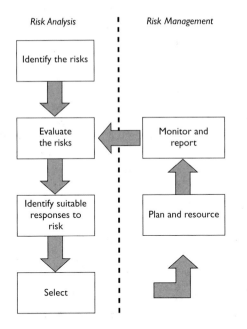

Figure 8.1

8.6   Risk analysis

8.6.1   Risk identification

This step identifies the potential risks (or opportunities) facing the project. Appendix G lists various categories of risk that make a useful start point for risk identification. It is important not to judge the likelihood of a risk at this early time. This is done in a controlled manner in a later step. Attempting to form judgements whilst 'brainstorming' a list of potential risks may lead to hurried and incorrect decisions to exclude some risks.

8.6.2   Risk evaluation

Risk evaluation is concerned with assessing probability and impact of individual risks, taking into account any interdependencies or other factors outside the immediate scope under investigation.

Probability is the evaluated likelihood of a particular outcome actually happening (including a consideration of the frequency with which the outcome may arise).

Impact is the evaluated effect or result of a particular outcome actually happening.

Impact should ideally be considered on:

- time
- cost
- quality
- scope
- benefit
- people.

For example, expensive damage to a building is relatively unlikely to happen, but would have enormous impact on business continuity. Conversely, occasional personal computer system failure is fairly likely to happen, but would not usually have a major impact on the business.

Some risks, such as financial risk, can be evaluated in numerical terms. Others, such as adverse publicity, can only be evaluated in subjective ways. There is a need for some framework for categorising risks. This book uses categories of *high, medium* and *low*.

8.6.2.1   Risk proximity

When considering a risk's probability, another aspect is when the risk might occur. The occurrence of some risks will be predicted to be further way in time than others, and so attention can be focused on the more immediate ones. This prediction is called the risk's proximity. The proximity of each risk should be included in the Risk Log.

8.6.3   Selection

The risk response process should involve identifying and evaluating a range of options for risk treatment, including the preparation and implementation of risk management plans. It is important that the control action put in place is proportional to the risk. Every control has an associated cost. The control action must offer value for money in relation to the risk that it is controlling.

Selection of the risk actions to take is a balance between a number of things, such as risk tolerance. For each possible action it is firstly a question of balancing the cost of taking that action against the likelihood and impact of allowing the risk to occur. As an example, if a charity carnival is arranged, is it worth taking out insurance for £3,000, guaranteeing £6,000 if the carnival is rained off? Or, since the carnival date is in summer, do we take the risk and not spend the insurance money?

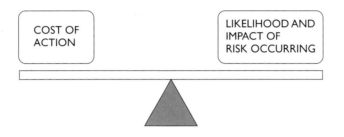

Figure 8.2

But the selection is usually more complex than that. As Figure 8.3 shows, there are many elements to be taken into consideration.

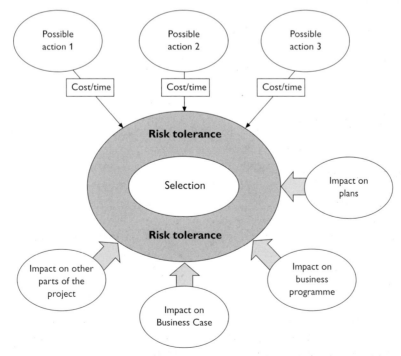

Figure 8.3

There may be several possible risk actions, each with different effects. The choice may be one of these options or a combination of two or more. We then have to consider the impact of (a) the risk occurring, and (b) the risk action on:

- the Team, Stage and/or Project Plans

- the business or programme

- the Business Case

- other parts of the project.

The consideration has to be done in the light of the risk tolerances.

8.6.4   Types of risk action

Risk actions fall broadly into five types:

Prevention	Terminate the risk – by doing things differently and thus removing the risk, where it is feasible to do so. Countermeasures are put in place that either stop the threat or problem from occurring, or prevent it having any impact on the project or business
Reduction	Treat the risk – take action to control it in some way where the actions either reduce the likelihood of the risk developing or limit the impact on the project to acceptable levels
Transference	This is a specialist form of risk reduction where the impact of the risk is passed to a third party via, for instance, an insurance policy or penalty clause
Acceptance	Tolerate the risk – perhaps because nothing can be done at a reasonable cost to mitigate it, or the likelihood and impact of the risk occurring are at an acceptable level
Contingency	These are actions planned and organised to come into force as and when the risk occurs

Any given risk could have appropriate actions in any or all of the above categories. There may be no cost-effective actions available to deal with a risk, in which case the risk must be accepted or the justification for the project revisited (to review whether the project is too risky to undertake).

The results of the risk evaluation activities are documented in the Risk Log. If the project is part of a programme, project risks should be examined for any impact on the programme (and vice versa). Where any cross-impact is found, the risk should be added to the other Risk Log.

8.7   Risk management

8.7.1   Planning and resourcing

Having made the selection, the implementation will need planning and resourcing, and is likely to include plan changes, new or modified Work Packages:

Planning, which, for the countermeasure actions itemised during the risk evaluation activities, consists of:

- identifying the quantity and type of resources required to carry out the actions
- developing a detailed plan of action; this will be included in Project and Stage Plans
- confirming the desirability of carrying out the actions identified during risk evaluation in light of any additional information gained
- obtaining management approval along with all the other aspects of the plans being produced.

Resourcing, which will identify and assign the actual resources to be used to conduct the work involved in carrying through the risk avoidance actions; these assignments will be shown in Stage and Team Plans. Note that the resources required for the prevention, reduction and transference actions will have to funded from the project budget since they are actions we are committed to carry out; contingent actions will normally be funded from a contingency budget.

8.7.2   Monitoring and reporting

There must be mechanisms in place for monitoring and reporting on the actions selected to address risks.

Some of the actions may have only been to monitor the identified risk for signs of a change in its status. Monitoring, however, may consist of:

- checking that execution of the planned actions is having the desired effect
- watching for the early warning signs that a risk is developing
- modelling trends, predicting potential risks or opportunities
- checking that the overall management of risk is being applied effectively.

Normally the risk 'owner' will have the responsibility of monitoring. If the owner is a Project Board member, the actual task of monitoring may be delegated, but the responsibility stays with the owner. The Executive, for example, has ultimate responsibility for monitoring any risks or opportunities facing the Business Case, particularly any external ones, such as changes in company policy. The Project Manager has the job of keeping a watching brief over all risks and checking that the defined actions, including monitoring, are taking place and are having the desired effect.

Risks owned at team level should have their status reported in the Checkpoint Reports. The Project Manager includes some form of report on any significant risks in the Highlight Report. The End Stage Report also summarises the risk status. Where a risk or opportunity actually occurs, a Project Issue should be used to trigger the necessary actions.

8.8 Mapping the risk management process to the P2 processes

At key points in a project, management of risk should be carried out, as shown in Figure 8.4.

8.8.1 Preparing a Project Brief (SU4)

The Risk Log needs to be created by this time. A suggested structure for this is given in Appendix B, Product Descriptions. The Project Mandate may have referred to a number of risks facing the potential project. These may be such risks as competitor action, impending or mooted legislation, company policy changes, staff reorganisation or cash-flow problems. Certainly, the preparation of the Project Brief should give rise to an early study of such risks. Creation of the Project Approach may also have introduced some extra risks.

8.8.2 Authorising Initiation (DP1)

This is the first formal moment when the Project Board can examine the Risk Log as part of deciding whether project initiation can be justified. Pragmatically, the Project Manager should have discussed informally with board members any known risks that seem to threaten the project viability.

8.8.3 Refining the Business Case and Risks (IP3)

The Project Manager examines risks again as part of preparing the Project Initiation Document. At this time the Project Plan will be created, and this may identify a number of project risks, such as unknown performance of resources, contractor ability and any assumptions being made in the plan. New risks may also come to light as a result of adding detail to the Project Brief. At the same time all existing risks are reviewed for any new information or change in their circumstances.

8.8.4 Authorising a Project (DP2)

The Project Board now has an updated Risk Log to examine as part of its decision on whether to go ahead with the project. As a result of refining the Business Case, a number of risks may have been identified. Very often the 'owners' of these risks will be members of the Project Board, and they should confirm their ownership and the actions required of them.

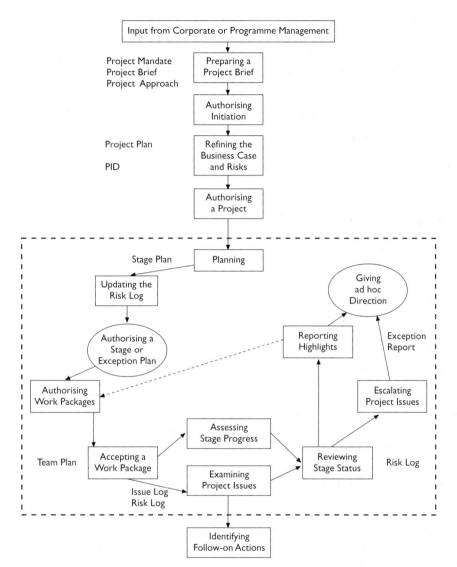

Figure 8.4 Risk flow, showing key points in a project when management is necessary

8.8.5   Planning (PL)

Each time a plan is produced, elements of the plan may identify new risks, modify existing ones or eliminate others. No plan should be put forward for approval before its risk content has been analysed (PL6). This analysis may lead to the plan being modified in order to take the appropriate risk action(s). The Risk Log should be updated with all such details.

8.8.6   Updating the Risk Log (SB4)

As part of his preparation for a new stage, the Project Manager updates the Risk Log with any changes to existing risks.

8.8.7   Authorising a Stage or Exception Plan (DP3)

Before authorising a plan, the Project Board has the opportunity to study the risk situation as part of its judgement of the continuing viability of the project.

8.8.8   Authorising a Work Package (CS1)

Negotiation with the Team Manager or team member may identify new risks or change old ones. It may require the Project Manager to go back and amend some part of the original Work Package or change the Stage Plan. Examples here are the assignee seeking more time or needing to change resources.

8.8.9   Accepting a Work Package (MP1)

This is the point when the Team Manager makes out a Team Plan to ensure that the products of the Work Package can be delivered within the constraints of the agreed Work Package. Like any other plan, it may contain new risks or modify existing ones.

8.8.10   Examining Project Issues (CS4)

Assessment of a new Project Issue may throw up a risk situation. This may stem from either the technical impact analysis or the business impact analysis. For example, the proposed change may produce a risk of pushing the stage or project beyond its tolerance margins.

8.8.11   Reviewing Stage Status (CS5)

This brings together the Stage Plan with its latest actual figures, the Project Plan, the Business Case, open Project Issues, the tolerance status and the Risk Log. The Project Manager (in conjunction with the Project Assurance roles) looks for risk situation changes as well as any other warning signs.

8.8.12   Escalating Project Issues (CS8)

As well as Project Issues, a risk change may cause the Project Manager to raise an Exception Report to the Project Board.

8.8.13   Reporting Highlights (CS6)

As part of this task, the Project Manager may take the opportunity to raise any risk matters with the Project Board. Examples here would be notifying the board of any risks that are no longer relevant, warning about new risks, and reminders about risks that board members should be keeping an eye on. The suggested format of a Highlight Report is included in Appendix B Product Description outlines.

8.8.14   Giving Ad Hoc Direction (DP4)

The Project Manager advises the Project Board of exception situations via the Exception Report. It has the opportunity to react with advice or a decision – for example, bringing the project to a premature close, requesting an Exception Plan, or removing the problem. The Project Board may instigate ad hoc advice on the basis of information given to it from corporate or programme management or another external source.

8.8.15   Identifying Follow-on Actions (CP2)

At the end of the project a number of risks may have been identified that will affect the product in its operational life. These should be transferred to the Follow-on Action Recommendations for the information of those who will support the product after the project.

9 CONFIGURATION MANAGEMENT

9.1 What is Configuration Management?

Configuration Management is a discipline which:

- registers all the products which are created as part of a project

- allocates identification and version numbers to all products

- controls access and change to the products of a project once they have been submitted to the configuration management system

- records the relationships between the various products, i.e. the products which form part of a sub-product, the common usage of a component, a bill of material of the final deliverable

- provides information on the status of products, including the author

- assists in the analysis of the impact of possible changes

- helps project management know what its assets are supposed to be, who is responsible for their development and whether the actual inventory of products matches the configuration records

- provides information on problem trends, such as which products are being changed regularly, thereby assisting in the proactive prevention of problems

- helps to control the distribution of changes to operational sites

- supports the maintenance of information on trusted releases to which products can revert in case of problems

- makes it more difficult for products to be changed maliciously, because all products are under the control of Configuration Management once they have been developed, thus improving security

- helps to recreate a release after any disaster by identifying the products required and their storage place

- gives project management the assurance that products are being developed in the correct sequence.

9.2 Possible problems

If products are defined at too low a level, the configuration librarian may be overwhelmed by the amount of data to be fed into the configuration library. This is particularly a problem where no configuration management software is being used.

If products are defined at too high a level, the information for impact analysis may be too vague and result in a larger than necessary product change being indicated, e.g. altering a whole sub-product when only one component is affected.

Procedures must cater for emergency changes, e.g. a call-out in the middle of the night, where a fix is required in order to let the operational product continue.

9.3   Configuration Management Plan

At the outset of a project the Project Manager must produce a plan, probably provided by the configuration librarian, of how products will be labelled, stored, tracked, reported on and issued. Part of this plan must show how changes will be controlled and implemented.

The Configuration Management Plan is part of the Project Quality Plan in the Project Initiation Document. It should contain at least the following sections:

■ Purpose of configuration management

There should be a brief description of what configuration management is, and its purpose in the project.

■ Role of configuration librarian

The first element is to allocate the role of librarian. The ideal is one individual to do the job, but where resources are tight or the project is small, it can be combined with another role. For example, in a small project such as a feasibility study, a team member may spend two hours a week to carry out the configuration librarian duties. Another possibility is that one person may perform the role for more than one project at a time.

■ Tools to be used

The next thing is to plan what tools (e.g. paper or card system or software package) will be used. This will impose most of the decisions on other parts of the plan, such as what method will be used and to what level the products will be recorded. The normal decision for the latter is to record down to the level of individually replaceable products. Other important factors are, of course, how much resource effort is available to do the recording and what software help is available.

■ Scope of configuration management

The plan will include definition of the scope of configuration management. What type of project products will be covered? Are the management products, such as plans, to be included? Will all specialist products be included or only the key deliverables?

■ Product attributes

Which attributes are to be recorded.

■ Identification Scheme

The method of identifying products, including how version numbering will be used.

- Product submission procedure

  How products are to be submitted to the librarian.

- Product issue procedure

  What procedure and form will be used to request the issue of a product held by the configuration librarian? What details will be kept of issue copies? How will genuine copies be identified? What will be done to recover copies when they are obsolete? How will products be moved back to development when they need to be changed?

- Baselines

  When baselines will be taken and for what reasons.

9.4   Product identification

In order to keep track of each product, a clear identification scheme must be adopted. Each product must be identified in a manner which is unique.

The unique identifier should consist of:

- project identifier
- product identifier
- version number.

9.4.1 Version numbers

The first version of a product comes under configuration management control when it is submitted to the librarian as being ready for quality review (or other form of quality checking). It usually keeps this version number as it moves through the verification and validation checks and becomes declared 'approved'. Whenever the product is later modified, a new version must be generated. This product must have the same name (identifier) as the original but with a new version reference. So a new version might be generated as a result of implementing Requests For Change or Off-Specifications which affect it or any product of which it consists.

Every time the product changes, the version number is incremented. This simple progression should be used whenever possible.

It is best to stick with the simple chain of sequential versions. This strategy has simple rules:

- there is only one 'latest version'
- modifications may be applied only to the latest version.

9.4.2   Physical labels

Every product needs to be physically labelled in some way to proclaim its identity. For documents, the label is usually just the name and version number written in the header. For a physical component it may be an identification tag or an identifier etched into it during manufacture. Approved documentation should have a coloured label. It should contain product name and number, copy number, version number and its shelf-life.

9.5   Product attributes

Part Number   A unique product identifier allocated by either the configuration management software or the librarian.

Title   The name of the product.

Description   This would be the Product Description, as required by PRINCE2, containing the fields:

- purpose
- composition
- derivation
- format
- skills required for its creation
- quality criteria
- quality review method
- checklist identity (where appropriate)
- quality checking skills required.

Current version   Number of this particular version of the product. This is usually linked to a baseline. You may wish to divide this into version and sub-version number, if you want to use, for example, '3.1'.

Category   This can identify the category of product, such as hardware, software, and documentation.

Source (especially if from an external source)

Serial no.   The serial number of any bought-in products.

Location   Where the product is physically kept.

Status   Current status of the product, for example:

- product in progress
- draft version available
- product under review
- product approved
- product withdrawn
- product superseded.

Other data that should be held under the 'status' heading are:

- start date of the current status
- project stage in which it will be developed
- responsible officer.

Parent   If a product has several components, the product is the 'parent' and the components 'children'. A 'child' can have only one 'parent'. This ensures that when you build a bill of material, a common component is only listed once.

Children   This shows links to any 'children', other sub-components which form part of it, and where this product is the one 'parent'.

Used in   Apart from the 'parent', this identifies any other product of which it forms a part.

Uses   Links to other products which form part of it, but of which it is not the 'parent'.

Change   Cross-references to Project Issues that affect it.

Quality review   Cross-reference to the quality file identifier where information about the quality review of the product is held.

9.6   Product submission and issue procedures

It is essential to control the input of products to the library and extraction of them from it.

9.6.1   Product submission

Authors of new or revised products should complete a product submission request form to the configuration librarian when they are satisfied that the product is complete and ready for review. It should contain at least:

- date of submission
- product identifier
- title
- version number (and sub-version number if applicable)

- status (this might default to draft version available)
- author.

If the product is a document, the librarian files it in a folder in the specialist file. If the product is in machine-readable form, the librarian should be provided with software procedures to transfer the product to an electronic library that can only be accessed by the librarian. Such procedures should remove the original from its development location (after validation of the transfer) to avoid unauthorised changes.

9.6.2   Product issue

There are several reasons why products require to be issued once they have been lodged with the librarian. While in draft form, copies of them may need to be sent to the Reviewers. Once they are approved, staff may need them to work on a later product, they may be the subject of an approved Project Issue or they may be released as part of a baseline.

Basically the same issue rules apply to both human- and machine-readable products. Master copies of products should never be issued, but held in the configuration libraries. The configuration librarian is responsible for maintaining a product issue record of:

- product identifier
- title
- version number
- recipient
- date of issue
- reason for the issue
- authority for the issue.

It is important to ensure that unregistered or obsolete copies are not inadvertently used to create either the product's next version or another product later in the life cycle (for example, using a superseded design document to build the product). It is therefore necessary to be able to clearly recognise what is an authorised copy.

Authorised copies should be stamped in colour. The lack of colour will indicate an unauthorised copy. The stamp should carry a date, where possible, after which it should not be taken as a copy of the current master without checking with the librarian.

Where a product copy has been taken for information, a quality review or any other short-term need, the librarian should try to follow up and recover unwanted copies for the reason mentioned in the previous paragraph.

When a new version is submitted, the librarian has the job of advising holders of copies of the old version. Again the old copies should be recalled and destroyed. It should not be taken for granted that a copy of the new version should be sent out to all holders. Their reason for holding a copy should be examined to see if it is required, or they should be asked if they still need a copy.

The configuration librarian should ensure that no product is issued for change to more than one person at any one time.

9.7   Status change

The developer is responsible for advising the configuration librarian of a status change.

9.8   Baseline

Baselines are moments in a product's evolution when it and all its components have reached an acceptable state, such that they can be 'frozen' and used as a base for the next step. The next step may be to release the product to the user, or it may be a design that will now be used to construct the products.

A baseline is created for one of a number of reasons:

- a sound base for future work
- as a point to which you can retreat if development goes wrong
- an indication of the component and version numbers of a release
- a bill of material showing the variants released to a specific site
- to copy the products and documentation at the current baseline to all remote sites
- a standard configuration (e.g. Product Description) against which supplies can be obtained (e.g. purchase of personal computers for a group)
- the state the product must reach before it can be released or upgraded
- comparison of one baseline against another in terms of the products contained and their versions
- transfer to another library
- the obtaining of a report on what products of the baseline are not of a specified status.

The baseline record itself should be a product, so that it can be controlled in the same way as other products. It is a baseline identifier, date, reason and list of all the products and their version numbers that comprise that baseline. Because of its different format it is often held in a separate file.

9.9   Building a release package

At the end of a project the product which has been developed is released into the live environment. The steps in building the release package are:

- identify the products to be included in the release
- ensure that all the required products have reached a status which allows them to be released into live operation
- report on any required products which do not have a current approved status
- build a release package
- list the changes since the previous release
- distribute the release
- be able to recreate any baseline (i.e. past release) if a site reports problems on an earlier release
- know which site has what version and variant of the product.

9.9.1   Control of releases

Each product release should have a release identifier, which identifies the baseline number.

9.9.2   Release package contents

A release should contain:

- the release name and identifier
- the release date
- the person/section/group with responsibility for the release. This will normally also be the contact for any installation problems. If not then this information should be added
- a brief description of the release, whether it is a complete or partial release, what has caused the release, its purpose, the major benefits over previous releases
- a list of prerequisites for the installation of the release
- a list of all the Project Issues answered by this release
- a bill of material, listing what is contained in the release
- installation steps. Again this should remind the installer of product back-ups and reversion procedures in case of trouble
- installation test steps
- any customisation steps. If the release can be tailored in any way, this describes the possibilities and lists the steps to be carried out
- notification of any dates when support for previous releases will cease
- an acknowledgement to be completed and returned by the installer on successful completion of the installation.

While current, a baseline cannot be changed. It remains active until it is superseded by the next baseline.

9.10   Configuration status accounting

Configuration status accounting provides a complete statement of the current status and history of the product. Its purpose is to provide a report on:

- the status of products
- all the events which have impacted the products.

In order to provide this information it is necessary for the configuration management method to record all the transactions affecting each product. At the simplest level this means that we can tell the status of each product and version.

For the purpose of status accounting the configuration management method should be able to produce reports on such things as:

- what is the history of development of a particular product
- who is responsible for this product
- what products in the design baseline have been changed since it was approved
- on what products have changes been approved but not yet implemented.

9.11   Configuration auditing

The purpose of configuration auditing is to account for the differences between a delivered product and its original agreed specification; to trace a path from the original specification through any approved changes to what a product looks like now.

A second aim of configuration auditing is to check that, in spite of changes which may have taken place, products conform to the latest agreed specification, and that quality inspection or test procedures have been performed satisfactorily. This is done by verifying at successive baselines that an item conforms to the specification produced for it at the previous baseline plus any approved changes.

These audits should check that:

- all authorised versions of products exist
- only authorised products exist
- all version changes are linked to Project Issue documents
- all Project Issue documents are correctly logged and authorised.

In PRINCE2 terms, this is defined as an inspection of the recorded Product Description and the current representation of that product to ensure that the latter matches its current specification, and that the specification of each product is consistent with that of its parent in the structure. In a sense, it can be regarded as similar to stock control. Does the book description match with what is on the shelf? In addition the audit should ensure that documentation is complete and that project standards have been met.

9.12   Configuration librarian role

9.12.1   Major functions

The major functions of the configuration librarian are:

- to plan, monitor and report on configuration management aspects
- to act as the focal point for configuration control.

9.12.2   Role description

The configuration librarian's role is to:

- assist the Project Manager to prepare the Configuration Management Plan
- help the Project Manager to create the configuration management structure and identification scheme
- assist in the identification of products
- create Product Description skeletons
- ensure that the structural relationship between products is known
- archive superseded products
- accept and record receipt of submission request forms with new or revised products into the configuration library
- act as custodian for master copies of all project products as defined in the Configuration Management Plan
- issue product copies for review, change, correction or information
- maintain copyholder information for both human- and machine-readable products.
- notify holders of any changes to their copies
- document a product's history so that traceability is assured if a product structure is changed during its life cycle. Wherever possible the product structure should not be changed unless it is to include additional items
- provide information for the assessment of the impact of a change to a product
- produce configuration status accounting reports
- assist in conducting configuration audits
- create baseline records as required
- produce release packages.

9.12.3   Jargon and abbreviations

Configuration management carries with it a certain amount of jargon and more than its share of initials. The following should clarify common terms and initials that will be used in the text.

9.12.3.1   *Configuration*

The set of all products which form part of the final product. Because of the huge effort needed to record and track all the products, in practice it usually refers to all products from the design onwards. For a software product the design would be broken down to the level of program specification, then source code, object code, manuals and test data.

9.12.3.2   *Configuration item record (product)*

One product which the project wants to track.

9.12.3.3   *Configuration librarian (CL)*

This is a person specifically appointed to perform the configuration management activities.

10 CHANGE CONTROL

In any project there will be changes for many reasons:

- the users change their mind on what is wanted
- the supplier finds that it will be impossible to deliver everything within the agreed schedule or cost
- the supplier cannot meet an acceptance criterion, such as performance
- a product delivered by an outside contractor or another product fails to meet its specification.
- government legislation changes and this must be reflected in the product specification.

All of these need a method to control them and their effect on the project. This method must make sure change requests are not ignored, but that nothing is implemented of which the project management is unaware. This includes the Project Board. In PRINCE2 all possible changes are handled by change control. Apart from controlling possible changes, it provides a formal entry point through which all questions can be raised. It is also a connecting link between quality reviews and the rest of the project:

- where an error which belongs to a different product than the one under review is found during quality review
- where work to correct an error found during quality review cannot be done during the agreed follow-up period.

10.1 Issue Log

The Issue Log is set up during initiation in the sub-process Setting Up Project Files (IP5). It records details of every issue raised and the current status.

10.2 Project Issues

There are three types of Project Issue in PRINCE2:

- Project Issues (questions or comments)
- Requests For Change
- Off-Specifications.

The standard way of dealing with all Project Issues is discussed in Chapter 5 on control. This chapter concentrates on those aspects linked to change control.

10.2.1   Request For Change

A Request For Change records a proposed modification to the user requirements or acceptance criteria (which were defined in the Project Initiation Document).

The Request For Change requires impact analysis to see how much work is involved. Senior team members with the appropriate skills and experience normally do this.

Note: When creating a Stage or Team Plan the planner should remember to make an allowance for impact analysis time, based on the volume of change requests expected.

The configuration librarian helps to identify what other products will be affected. It is particularly important that the librarian identifies any baselined products that will need to change. This is because the Project Board has already been told of the completion of those products. The Project Board must approve any change to such products.

The identified work is costed and the impact on the Stage and/or Team Plan's budget and schedule assessed. For the next decision the Project and/or Team Manager will want to know if any of the work could be done within the tolerance levels of the current plan. For this reason it is best that a batch of requests are studied, to give a wider view of the effect on the plans.

In preparation for the next decision, the Requests For Change have to be awarded a priority rating. PRINCE2 suggests that this can be one of four:

- mandatory: the product will not work or will not do the required job without this change
- highly desirable: it will be possible to work around the lack of this change, but it will be inefficient to do so and the absence of this change can only be tolerated for a short period of time
- nice-to-have: this change does not affect the working of the product, but would improve it in a small way
- cosmetic: this change only affects the appearance of some aspect of the product, but not its performance.

It should be the job of the Senior User to provide the priority rating and discuss the proposed change with the users.

In order for the Request For Change to be implemented, it must be approved by either the Project Manager or the Project Board. Whose decision it is depends on the following:

- If it is a change to a product that has not already been baselined and the work can be done within the current plan's tolerances, the Project Manager can make the decision to implement it. Alternatively it can be passed to the Project Board for its decision. Since experience shows that there will be a lot of changes during the project, it is a good idea to make the Project Board decide on any changes other than trivialities. This keeps the board aware of how many changes are being requested and their cumulative impact on the schedule and cost.

- If the change is to one or more products that the Project Board has already been told are complete (to any baseline, not necessarily the final one), the decision must be made by the Project Board. More than anything, this is to retain the confidence level of the board. If it has been told that something is finished and later finds out that it has been changed without consultation, its sense of being in control evaporates.

- If the work to do the Request For Change cannot be done within the tolerance levels of the current Stage Plan, the decision on action must come from the Project Board. The Project Manager must submit an Exception Report with the Request For Change, listing the available options and making a recommendation.

The Project Manager passes to the Project Board all those Requests For Change which have not been decided by the Project Manager. This is done in the sub-process Escalating Project Issues (CS8). It is the Project Board's job to put them in order of priority. This consideration is part of the sub-process Giving Ad Hoc Direction (DP4).

The Project Board's decision may be to:

- implement the change. If the change required an Exception Plan, then this means requesting and approving an Exception Plan
- delay the change to an enhancement project after the current one is finished
- defer a decision until a later meeting
- ask for more information
- cancel the request.

The decision should be documented on the request and the Issue Log.

Whenever a Project Issue's status changes, a copy should be sent to the originator.

The Project Manager is responsible for scheduling any approved changes. This work will possibly involve the issue of a copy of one or more products by the configuration librarian.

On receipt of a completed Request For Change the configuration librarian should ensure that any amended products have been resubmitted to the configuration library. The quality file should be updated with the finalised request, the Issue Log annotated and the originator advised.

10.2.2   Off-Specification

An Off-Specification is used to document any situation where the product fails to meet its specification in some respect.

The configuration librarian allocates the next unique Project Issue identifier from the log, sends a copy of the issue to its author. Senior team members with the help of the configuration librarian carry out an impact analysis to discover which products are affected by the Off-Specification, and then assess the effort needed to correct the problem.

If it is discovered that the Off-Specification has been raised in error, and should have been a Request For Change, the Project Issue is suitably commented, the Issue Log is updated and the originator informed.

As with Requests For Change, the decision on action is taken by either the Project Manager or Project Board:

■ If the Off-Specification does not involve a change to a product which has already been baselined and the work can be done within the current plan's tolerances, the Project Manager can make the decision to implement it

■ If the Off-Specification requires changes to one or more products which the Project Board have already been told are complete (to any baseline, not necessarily the final one), the decision must be made by the Project Board

■ If the work to do the Off-Specification cannot be done within the tolerance levels of the current Stage Plan, the decision on action must come from the Project Board. The Project Manager must submit an Exception Report with the Off-Specification Report, offering options and making a recommendation.

The Project Board's decision may be to:

■ correct the fault. If the work required an Exception Plan, then this means approving the Exception Plan (using the sub-process Authorising a Stage or Exception Plan (DP3))

■ delay correction of the fault to an enhancement project after the current one is finished

■ defer a decision until a later meeting

■ ask for more information.

The decision should be documented on the Off-Specification and the Issue Log, and an updated copy filed. Whenever its status changes, a copy of the issue should be sent to the originator.

The Project Manager is responsible for scheduling any approved work to correct Off-Specifications. This work will possibly involve the issue of a copy of one or more products by the configuration librarian.

On receipt of a corrected Off-Specification, the configuration librarian should ensure that any amended products have been resubmitted to the configuration library. The Issue Log should be updated with the final details and the originator advised.

10.2.3   Delegation to a Change Authority

The Project Board has the option to delegate consideration of change requests to a separate Change Authority. This is normally a body representing the Senior User.

This usually happens when more change requests are expected than the Project Board has time to handle. A budget must be handed to the Change Authority to pay for any approved changes. Restrictions are placed on the group in terms of how much of the budget can be spent in any one stage or on any single change without reference back to the Project Board.

The appointment of this authority should happen in the initiation stage and be documented as part of the change control description.

11 PRODUCT-BASED PLANNING

PRINCE uses a product-based planning technique. There are two reasons for this. The products have to be identified in order to consider what activities are needed in order to produce those products. The quality of a product can be measured and therefore planned; whereas the quality of an activity can only be measured by the quality of its outcome (the product).

The product-based planning technique is used by the process Defining and Analysing Products (PL2) in the common process Planning.

Product-based planning has three components:

- Product Breakdown Structure
- Product Descriptions
- Product Flow Diagram.

11.1 Product Breakdown Structure (PBS)

Most planning methods begin a plan by thinking of the activities, and listing these in a hierarchical structure called a Work Breakdown Structure (WBS). PRINCE believes that the activities depend on what products are required to be produced, and that the correct start point for a plan is to list the products.

A Product Breakdown Structure is a hierarchy of the required products. At the top is the final end product, e.g. procured office equipment, a new washing machine, a department moved from one location to another. This product is then broken down into its major constituents at the next level. Each constituent is then broken down into its parts, and this process continues until the planner has reached the level of detail required for the plan.

Another important departure from other methods is the PRINCE emphasis that, apart from the specialist products of a project, there are always management and quality products. Listing these will remind us that they need effort and time to produce and therefore need to be planned as much as the production of specialist products.

11.2 Product Description

For each identified product, at all levels of the Product Breakdown Structure, a description is produced. Its creation forces the planner to consider if sufficient is known about the product in order to plan its production. It is also the first time that the quality of the product is considered. The quality criteria indicate how much and what type of quality checking will be required.

The purposes of this are, therefore, to provide a guide:

- to the planner in how much effort will be required to create the product
- to the author of the product on what is required
- against which the finished product can be measured.

These descriptions are a vital checklist to be used at a quality check of the related products.

The description should contain:

- the purpose of the product
- the products from which it is derived
- the composition of the product
- any standards for format and presentation
- the quality criteria to be applied to the product
- the quality verification method to be used.

The Product Description is given to both the product's creator and those who will verify its quality.

11.3   Product Flow Diagram (PFD)

The Product Flow Diagram is a diagram showing how a product is derived from another product or group of products.

11.4   Product-based Planning example

A simple example is given in order to explain the PRINCE product-based planning technique. Please note – the example project is a very simple one, chosen so that the reader can concentrate on understanding the technique. What follows are the product-based planning steps for the procurement and installation of some office equipment. The final output from this technique would feed into the remainder of the planning steps described in the Planning (PL) process.

11.4.1   Product Breakdown Structure example

If we start with 'procured office equipment' at the top of hierarchy, we then break this down to the major products. Figure 11.1 gives an example of what this might look like. There is not necessarily one right answer. The whole technique is trying to jog your memory about what will be needed.

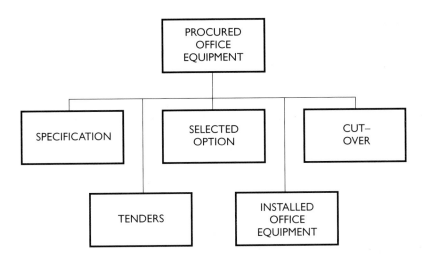

Figure 11.1 Product Breakdown Structure start

Each of the second level products is now broken down into its constituent products. Figure 11.2 shows what the PBS might look like developed down to three levels.

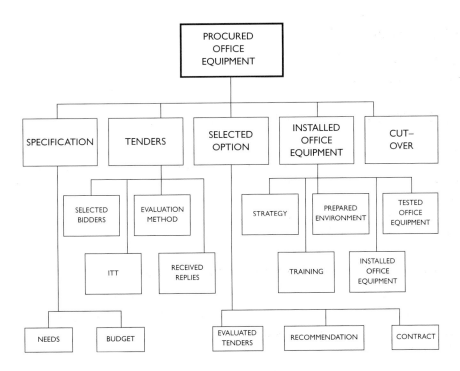

Figure 11.2 Product Breakdown Structure completed

This breakdown process continues until the planner has reached a level of detail appropriate for the plan to be produced. As a rule of thumb, three levels is often enough for a Project Plan.

11.4.2   Management products

Having thought of the technical products, management products should be listed. Management products include any contracts, all plans, control documents, progress reports, meeting minutes and approvals, quality checking documents and Product Descriptions. An important management control at the beginning of every project is project initiation, where it is checked that justification of the project exists and everyone knows his or her responsibilities.

For this example the management products might look like those in Figure 11.3. PRINCE offers a general list of these products that can be used unchanged for most projects.

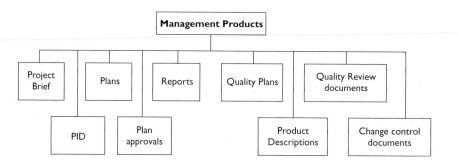

Figure 11.3 Management products example

11.4.3   Create Product Descriptions

A Product Description for the recommendation in the example would look like the following:

Title   Office Equipment Recommendation

Purpose   To document a recommended course of action to the Project Board in response to the evaluation of tenders for the supply of office equipment.

Content

- reference to the specification
- management summary
- list of tenders evaluated
- recommended tender and reasons
- way forward.

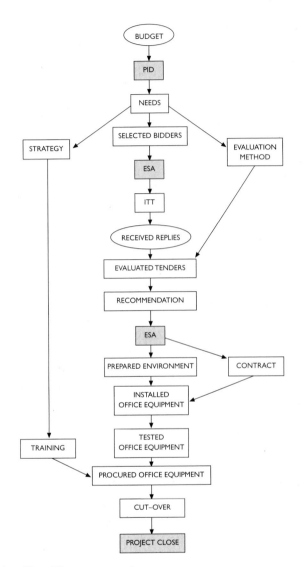

Figure 11.4 Product Flow Diagram example

Derivation

- tenders
- evaluations
- specification.

Quality criteria

- reflects evaluation of all the tenders
- makes the reasons for the recommendation clear

- recommendation relates to the priorities of the specification
- clarifies the next steps to be taken.

Quality Verification Method   Formal quality review by Project Assurance roles.

11.4.4 Product Flow Diagram example

Time flows in one direction only, top to bottom or left to right, depending on the paper or other drawing medium available. Figure 11.4 begins with the specialist products, and considers what is available at the start of the project and ends with the required final products. All products to be created by the project are shown in boxes. Drawing an arrow to a product from each of the products from which it is derived shows the dependencies of a product. Any products that are expected to be already available or coming from outside sources are shown in an ellipse.

In tracing the product flow in this way, extra interim products may be identified which are required to build and support the final products. Products that exist outside the project and are needed in the building of the new products will also be discovered. For example, a feasibility study for it may have already been done as part of the overall strategy work, or a description of the current product may already exist. Any extra products discovered in this way are added to the Product Breakdown Structure.

After putting all the specialist products into the Product Flow Diagram, the management products are examined to see if they should be brought into the flow. Products such as contracts and End Stage Assessments should be added to the diagram. Quality products are normally brought in at a low level of detail, therefore they tend to appear in Stage or Team Plans, rather than Project Plans.

12 QUALITY REVIEW

A quality review is a team method of assuring a document's quality by a review process. The purpose of the review is for peers of the person who created the product to inspect the product for errors in a planned, independent, controlled and documented manner and ensure that any errors found are fixed.

12.1 Aim

The major aim is to improve product quality. There are several other aims. These are to:

- trap errors as early as possible
- encourage the concept of products as team property rather than belonging to an individual
- enhance product status data (i.e. not only has the creator declared it finished, but others have confirmed that it is of good quality)
- monitor the use of standards
- spread knowledge of the product among those whose own products may interact with it.

Quality review documentation is filed in the quality file. With the Quality Log it provides a record that the product was inspected, that any errors found were corrected and that the corrections were themselves checked.

12.2 Roles at the quality review

The interests of parties who should be considered when drawing up the list of attendees are:

- the product's producer
- the Project Board
- those with assurance responsibilities delegated by the Project Board
- the customer
- staff who will operate or maintain the finished product
- staff from other systems which will be affected by the product
- independent observers (such as quality assurance).

The roles involved in the quality review process are:

- The Producer, who is the author of the product being reviewed. This role has to ensure that the Reviewers have all the required information in order to perform their job. This means getting a copy of the product to them during the preparation phase, plus any other documents needed to put it in context, then answering questions about the product during the review until a decision can be reached on whether there is an error or not. Finally the Producer will do most, if not all, of the correcting work. The Producer must not be allowed to be defensive about the product.

■ The Chairman. In choosing the person for this role, consideration must be given to the attitude of the Producer if that person's manager is to be present. An open, objective attitude is needed. Required attributes are:

☐ be a project member but not the product author

☐ have technical knowledge of the product

☐ have sufficient authority to control the review

☐ have chairmanship experience.

The Chairman is responsible for ensuring that the quality review is properly organised and that it runs smoothly during all of its phases.

For the Preparation phase this includes checking that administrative procedures have been carried out and that the right people have been invited. If there is a Project Support function, this administration can be delegated.

■ The Reviewers, who must be competent to assess the product from their particular viewpoints.

■ The Scribe, who records any errors which need to be corrected. Quality reviews can be run without this role. In such cases, the Chairman does it. It can, however, be difficult for the Chairman to keep control of a meeting with a number of Reviewers while he or she is making a note of an error found in the document. If the note-taking can be allocated to a Scribe, this allows the Chairman to concentrate on controlling the review. If the project is big enough to have a Project (or programme) Support group, it is useful to train one or more resources from there in the role of Scribe. Smaller projects have to consider whether the costs of a separate Scribe can be justified.

It must be remembered that these are roles. They must all be present at a quality review, but a person may take on more than one role.

12.3   Quality review phases

There are three distinct phases within the quality review procedure:

■ preparation

■ review

■ follow-up.

12.3.1   Preparation

The objective of this phase is for the Reviewers to examine the product and create a list of questions for the review.

The Chairman checks with the Producer that the product will be ready on time. If not, the Project Manager is advised, leading to an update of the Stage Plan. The Reviewers should have been planned at Stage Planning time. This should be one of the major functions of the assurance roles. The Chairman ensures that the Reviewers are still available, and that the venue has been arranged.

An invitation is sent out, giving the time and place for the review with copies of the product, the relevant Product Description and any checklist available. This should be done sufficiently early that the Reviewers have time to examine the document before the review and provide a Question List to the Chairman.

Each Reviewer studies the product and supporting documents (particularly the quality criteria included in the Product Description), annotates the product, and completes a Question List.

A copy of the Question Lists should, wherever possible, be sent to the Chairman before the review. Producer and Chairman should review these lists in order to set up an agenda. To save time at the review, the Producer can identify in advance any errors pointed out on the Question Lists with which he or she agrees.

12.3.2   Review

The objective of the review is to review the Question Lists and agree any actions needed to correct or complete the product.

The Producer and the Reviewers discuss each item on the agenda in turn. To save time, there should be no discussion on parts of the document which have not caused questions.

The Chairman controls the discussion, ensuring that no solutions are discussed (other than obvious and immediately accepted solutions!) and that the review does not get bogged down in interminable arguments. The policy should be 'If there is disagreement after everyone has had their say, then it's an action item.' Follow-up Actions are noted on an Action List by the Scribe. No other minutes are taken of the review.

At the conclusion of the review, the Chairman asks the Scribe to read back the Follow-up Actions and determines responsibility for correction of any points. A target date is set for each action and the initials of the person who will sign off each correction as acceptable are recorded on the Follow-up Action List by the Scribe. This sign-off may be by the Reviewer who raised the query initially, but other Reviewers have the option of checking the correction.

The Chairman lastly seeks the Reviewers' and Producer's opinions on the outcome of the review. There can be one of three normal outcomes:

- the product is error-free
- the product will be acceptable on completion of the actions noted
- there is so much corrective work to be done that the entire product needs to be reviewed from scratch.

The Chairman will advise the Project Manager of the outcome, so that the Stage Plan can be updated. A result notification will be completed and the documents attached. These forms will be filed in the quality file and the Quality Log updated.

The Reviewers' Question Lists, copies of the product (probably containing the Reviewer's annotations) and any other relevant documentation is collected by the Scribe and passed to the Producer to assist in the Follow-up. This may cause an update to configuration management records in two ways. Firstly, the status of the product should be updated. Secondly, details of who has copies will now need to be revised.

12.3.3   Follow-up

The objective of the last phase is to ensure that all actions identified on the Follow-up Action List are dealt with.

Those identified in the Follow-up Action List now make the corrections. This will normally be the Producer, but other staff may have been identified to do some of the work.

When an error has been fixed, the Scribe will obtain sign-off from whoever is nominated on the Follow-up Action List. When all errors have been corrected and sign-off obtained, the Scribe gives the Follow-up Action List to the Chairman, who confirms that the product is complete. The Follow-up Action List is filed in the quality file, and the Quality Log and the Stage Plan updated.

12.4   Quality review steps

12.4.1   Chairman

12.4.1.1   Preparation phase

- Check with the Producer that the product is ready for review.
- If not, advise the Project Manager of the revised completion date.
- Confirm that the planned Reviewers are still available. If not, ask the Project Manager and assurance roles to identify replacements.
- Agree with the Producer and Reviewers the amount of preparation time required.

- Arrange a date, time, venue and duration for the review.

- Advise the Project Manager if there is to be any delay in holding the review.

- Arrange for copies of relevant documents to be provided.

- Ensure the configuration librarian provides product copies, Product Descriptions and any relevant checklist or standard for all Reviewers.

- Send an invitation with the documentation to each Reviewer, with a copy to the Producer.

- Decide if a short overview presentation of the product to the Reviewers is required prior to the review, and arrange it if it is.

- Arrange with the Reviewers for return of their Question Lists prior to the review.

- Create an agenda for the review from the Question Lists in consultation with the Producer. Agree any obvious errors with the Producer. Prioritise the questions and roughly allocate time.

- Confirm attendance with each Reviewer shortly before the review. If a Reviewer cannot attend, ensure that the Reviewer's Question List is submitted. If too many Reviewers cannot attend, reschedule the review and inform the Project Manager.

12.4.1.2   Review

- Provide a copy of the agenda to all attendees.

- Open the review, stating objectives and apologising for any non-attendees.

- Decide whether the Reviewers present and the Question Lists from any unable to attend are adequate to review the product. If not, the review should be stopped, rescheduled and the Project Manager advised.

- Identify any errors already agreed by the Producer and ensure that these are documented on the Follow-up Action List.

- Step through the agenda, with the appropriate Reviewer enlarging where necessary on the question.

- Allow reasonable discussion on each question between Producer and Reviewers to decide if action is required.

- Ensure that any agreed actions are documented on a Follow-up Action List.

- Prevent any discussion of possible solutions or matters of style.

- Ensure every Reviewer is given a chance to voice their comments.

- Where agreement cannot be reached on a point in a reasonable time frame, declare it an action point and ensure that the Reviewer(s) concerned are noted.

- Where appropriate, decide on the premature close of the review in the light of the comments made.

- If faults are identified in products other than the one under review, ensure that a Project Issue is raised.

- Ensure that any annotated products detailing minor or typographical errors are collected and passed to the Producer.

- Have the Follow-up Action List read back and obtain confirmation from the Producer and Reviewers that it is complete and correct.

- Identify who is to be involved in working on each action item. Obtain a target date for completion of the work.

- Agree with the Reviewers who is to approve the work done on each action item and ensure that this is noted on the Follow-up Action List.

- Pass the Follow-up Action List and all copies of the annotated product to the Producer. Lodge a copy of the Follow-up Action List in the quality file.

- Decide with the Reviewers what the status of the review is. It can be:

  - ☐ complete with no errors discovered

  - ☐ complete with some rework required

  - ☐ in need of rework and another review.

- If the review is incomplete, recommend a course of action to the Project Manager. There are five possible courses of action. The last two of these should only be used in order to meet unavoidable deadlines, and are not recommended:

  - ☐ the product should be revised and submitted to another review

  - ☐ the review should be reconvened to finish with no need for interim re-work

  - ☐ the review should be reconvened with a different set of Reviewers without revising the product

  - ☐ the review should be declared complete, the errors found so far corrected and the rest of the product accepted without further question

  - ☐ the review should be abandoned and the product used without change, i.e. none of the errors corrected, but noted in a Project Issue Report.

12.4.1.3   Follow-up

- Monitor the correction of errors and sign off the Follow-up Action List when all corrections have been approved.

- If an action cannot be taken within the time allowed, the Chairman and Producer may decide to transfer it to a Project Issue as a possible Off-Specification. This requires the agreement of the Project Manager. The Follow-up Action List item is closed with the Project Issue log number and those waiting to sign off the action item informed.

- On completion and sign-off of all action items, sign off the Follow-up Action List as complete and have it filed in the quality file with copies to all Reviewers. Update the Quality Log.

- Supervise the passage of the error-free product to the configuration librarian.

12.4.2   Producer's responsibilities

12.4.2.1   Preparation

- Ask the Project Manager to nominate a Chairman if none is identified in the Stage Plan.

- Confirm with the Chairman that the product is ready for review. This should occur several days prior to the planned review date to allow for preparation time.

- Confirm the attendees with the Chairman and the Project Assurance Team.

- Agree with the Chairman and Reviewers the length of preparation time needed.

- Assess the Question Lists from the Reviewers, identifying any errors in the product that can be agreed without further discussion.

- Agree the agenda with the Chairman in the light of the Question Lists.

12.4.2.2   Review

- Answer any questions from the Reviewers about the product.

- Offer an opinion to the Chairman on whether a question has highlighted an error in the product.

- When the review ends, collect from the Scribe the Follow-up Action List and any annotated copies of the product from the Reviewers.

12.4.2.3   Follow-up

- Resolve all allocated action items.

- Obtain sign-off for each action item from the nominated Reviewers.

- Inform the Chairman if the resolution of the action items cannot be completed within the time allowed and agree new target dates.

- If an action item cannot be resolved within the time allowed, then ask the Chairman if it may be transferred to a Project Issue.

- Pass the Follow-up Action List to the Scribe on resolution of all the action items.

12.4.3   Reviewer's responsibilities

12.4.3.1   Preparation

- Consult the Product Description and any pertinent checklists and standards against which the product should be judged.
- Allow sufficient time to prepare for the review.
- Consult any necessary source documents from which the product is derived.
- Annotate any spelling or typographical mistakes on the product copy (but do not add these to the Question List).
- Check the product for completeness, defects, ambiguities, inconsistencies and lack of clarity, or deviations from standards. Note any such items on the Question List.
- Forward the Question List to the Chairman in advance of the review. If possible, this should be done early enough to give the Chairman time to prepare an agenda and for the Producer to digest the points.
- Forward a Question List and the annotated product copy to the Chairman if unable to attend the review.

12.4.3.2   Review

- Ensure that the points noted on your Question List are raised at the review.
- Restrict comments to faults in the product under review.
- Avoid attempting to redesign the product.
- Avoid 'improvement' comments if the product meets requirements and standards.
- Verify and approve the Follow-up Action List as complete and correct when read back by the Scribe.
- Agree to assist in the resolution of any action items if requested by the Chairman.
- Request to check and sign off any action items either raised personally or which impact your area of expertise or interest.

12.4.3.3   Follow-up

- Work with the Producer to resolve any allocated action items.
- Check and sign off those action items where allocated as approver.

12.4.4   Scribe

- Document any agreed actions on a Follow-up Action List.

- Collect and pass any annotated products detailing minor or typographical errors to the Producer.

- Read back the Follow-up Action List on request.

- Note on the Follow-up Action List who is to approve the work done on each action item.

- Lodge a copy of the Follow-up Action List in the quality file. Pass the Follow-up Action List and all copies of the annotated product to the Producer.

- Keep the Chairman informed of the status of the review.

12.5   Formal and informal reviews

Quality reviews can be either formal (i.e. a scheduled meeting conducted as described above) or informal (i.e. a 'get-together' between two or three people to informally walk through a product). Informal quality reviews will follow the same format as a formal quality review – the paperwork resulting from both meetings is the same. The main difference will be the informality of the proceedings during the three phases and the overall time required.

In informal quality reviews two or three people can be given the task of checking each other's work on a regular basis. Alternatively, an experienced person can be asked to hold reviews of the work of one or two inexperienced people.

Factors in deciding whether a formal or informal review is needed are:

- the importance of the product

- whether it is a final deliverable

- whether it is the source for a number of other products

- the author's experience

- who the product's consumer is.

12.6   Summary

The PRINCE quality review technique is a structured way of running a meeting to ensure that all aspects are properly covered. It needs to be used with common sense to avoid the dangers of an over-bureaucratic approach but with intent to follow the procedures laid down.

APPENDIX A
ROLE DESCRIPTIONS

A.1   Project Board

A.1.1   General

The Project Board is appointed by corporate or programme management to provide overall direction and management of the project. The Project Board is accountable for the success of the project, and has responsibility and authority for the project within the remit (the Project Mandate) set by corporate or programme management.

The Project Board is the project's 'voice' to the outside world and is responsible for any publicity or other dissemination of information about the project.

A.1.2   Specific responsibilities

The Project Board approves all major plans and authorises any major deviation from agreed Stage Plans. It is the authority that signs off the completion of each stage as well as authorises the start of the next stage. It ensures that required resources are committed and arbitrates on any conflicts within the project or negotiates a solution to any problems between the project and external bodies. In addition, it approves the appointment and responsibilities of the Project Manager and any delegation of its Project Assurance responsibilities.

The Project Board has the following responsibilities. It is a general list and will need tailoring for a specific project.

At the beginning of the project:

- assurance that the Project Initiation Document complies with relevant customer standards and policies, plus any associated contract with the supplier
- agreement with the Project Manager on that person's responsibilities and objectives
- confirmation with corporate or programme management of project tolerances
- specification of external constraints on the project such as quality assurance
- approval of an accurate and satisfactory Project Initiation Document
- delegation of any Project Assurance roles
- commitment of project resources required by the next Stage Plan.

As the project progresses:

- provision of overall guidance and direction to the project, ensuring it remains within any specified constraints
- review of each completed stage and approval of progress to the next
- review and approval of Stage Plans and any Exception Plans
- 'ownership' of one or more of the identified project risks as allocated at plan approval time, i.e. the responsibility to monitor the risk and advise the Project Manager of any change in its status and to take action, if appropriate, to ameliorate the risk
- approval of changes
- compliance with corporate or programme management directives.

At the end of the project:

- assurance that all products have been delivered satisfactorily
- assurance that all acceptance criteria have been met
- approval of the End Project Report
- approval of the Lessons Learned Report and the passage of this to the appropriate standards group to ensure action
- decisions on the recommendations for follow-on actions and the passage of these to the appropriate authorities
- arrangements, where appropriate, for a Post Project Review
- project closure notification to corporate or programme management.

The Project Board owns the process 'Directing a Project'.

The Project Board is ultimately responsible for assurance that the project remains on course to deliver the desired outcome of the required quality to meet the Business Case defined in the Project Initiation Document. According to the size, complexity and risk of the project, the Project Board may decide to delegate some of this Project Assurance responsibility. Later in this appendix Project Assurance is defined in more detail.

One Project Board responsibility that should receive careful consideration is that of approving and funding changes. Chapter 10 on change control should be read before finalising this responsibility of approving and funding changes.

Responsibilities of specific members of the Project Board are described in the respective sections below.

A.2   Executive

A.2.1   General

The Executive is ultimately responsible for the project, supported by the Senior User and Senior Supplier. The Executive has to ensure that the project is value for money, ensuring a cost-conscious approach to the project, balancing the demands of business, user and supplier.

Throughout the project the Executive 'owns' the Business Case.

A.2.2   Specific responsibilities

The specific responsibilities of the Executive should be to:

- ensure that a tolerance is set for the project in the Project Brief
- authorise customer expenditure and set stage tolerances
- approve the End Project Report and Lessons Learned Report
- brief corporate or programme management about project progress
- organise and chair Project Board Meetings
- recommend future action on the project to corporate or programme management if the project tolerance is exceeded
- approve the sending of the notification of project closure to corporate or programme management.

The Executive is responsible for overall business assurance of the project, i.e. that it remains on target to deliver products which will achieve the expected business benefits, and that it will complete within its agreed tolerances for budget and schedule. Business assurance covers:

- validation and monitoring of the Business Case against external events and against project progress
- keeping the project in line with customer strategies
- monitoring project finance on behalf of the customer
- monitoring the business risks to ensure that these are kept under control
- monitoring any supplier and contractor payments
- monitoring changes to the Project Plan to see if there is any impact on the needs of the business or the project Business Case;
- assessing the impact of potential changes on the Business Case and Project Plan
- constraining user and supplier excesses

■ informing the project of any changes caused by a programme of which the project is part (this responsibility may be transferred if there is other programme representation on the Project Management Team)

■ monitoring stage and project progress against the agreed tolerance.

If the project warrants it, the Executive may delegate some responsibility for the above business assurance functions.

A.3   Senior User

A.3.1   General

The Senior User is responsible for the specification of the needs of all those who will use the final product(s), user liaison with the project team and for monitoring that the solution will meet those needs within the constraints of the Business Case.

The role represents the interests of all those who will use the final product(s) of the project, those for whom the product will achieve an objective, or those who will use the product to deliver benefits. The Senior User role commits user resources and monitors products against requirements. This role may require more than one person to cover all the user interests. For the sake of effectiveness the role should not be split between too many people.

A.3.2   Specific responsibilities

Responsibilities of the Senior User are to:

■ ensure the desired outcome of the project is specified

■ make sure that progress towards the outcome required by the users remains consistent from the user perspective

■ promote and maintain focus on the desired project outcome

■ ensure that any user resources required for the project are made available

■ approve Product Descriptions for those products which act as inputs or outputs (interim or final) from the supplier function, or will affect them directly and ensure that the products are signed off once completed

■ prioritise and contribute user opinions on Project Board decisions on whether to implement recommendations on proposed changes

■ resolve user requirements and priority conflicts

■ provide the user view on recommended Follow-up Actions

■ brief and advise user management on all matters concerning the project.

The assurance responsibilities of the Senior User are that:

- specification of the user's needs is accurate, complete and unambiguous
- development of the solution at all stages is monitored to ensure that it will meet the user's needs and is progressing towards that target
- impact of potential changes is evaluated from the user point of view
- risks to the users are constantly monitored
- testing of the product at all stages has the appropriate user representation
- quality control procedures are used correctly to ensure products meet user requirements
- user liaison is functioning effectively.

Where the project's size, complexity or importance warrants it, the Senior User may delegate the responsibility and authority for some of the assurance responsibilities to a user assurance role.

A.4   Senior Supplier

A.4.1   General

The Senior Supplier represents the interests of those designing, developing, facilitating, procuring, implementing, operating and maintaining the project products. The Senior Supplier role must have the authority to commit or acquire supplier resources required.

It should be noted that in some environments the customer may share design authority or have a major say in it.

If necessary more than one person may be required to represent the suppliers.

A.4.2   Specific responsibilities

The Senior Supplier's specific responsibilities are to:

- agree objectives for specialist activities
- make sure that progress towards the outcome remains consistent from the supplier perspective
- promote and maintain focus on the desired project outcome from the point of view of supplier management
- ensure that the supplier resources required for the project are made available
- approve Product Descriptions for specialist products
- contribute supplier opinions on Project Board decisions on whether to implement recommendations on proposed changes

- resolve supplier requirements and priority conflicts
- arbitrate on, and ensure resolution of any specialist priority or resource conflicts
- brief non-technical management on specialist aspects of the project.

The Senior Supplier is responsible for the specialist integrity of the project. The specialist assurance role responsibilities are to:

- advise on the selection of specialist strategy, design and methods
- ensure that any specialist and operating standards defined for the project are met and used to good effect
- monitor potential changes and their impact on the correctness, completeness and integrity of products against their Product Description from a specialist perspective
- monitor any risks in the specialist and production aspects of the project
- ensure quality control procedures are used correctly so that products adhere to specialist requirements.

If warranted, some of this assurance responsibility may be delegated to separate specialist assurance personnel. Depending on the particular customer/supplier environment of a project, the customer may also wish to appoint people to specialist assurance roles.

A.5   Project Manager

A.5.1   General

The Project Manager has the authority to run the project on a day-to-day basis on behalf of the Project Board within the constraints laid down by the board. In a customer/supplier environment the Project Manager will normally come from the customer organisation, but there will be projects where the Project Manager comes from the supplier. A typical example would be an in-house project, where the customer and supplier belong to the same organisation. In the latter case, the customer may appoint a 'Project Director' or 'Controller' to be its day-to-day liaison with the Project Manager.

The Project Manager's prime responsibility is to ensure that the project produces the required products, to the required standard of quality and within the specified constraints of time and cost. The Project Manager is also responsible for the project producing a result which is capable of achieving the benefits defined in the Business Case.

A.5.2   Specific responsibilities

The Project Manager's specific responsibilities are to:

- manage the production of the required products
- direct and motivate the project team

- plan and monitor the project

- agree any delegation and use of Project Assurance roles required by the Project Board

- produce the Project Initiation Document

- prepare Project, Stage and, if necessary, Exception Plans in conjunction with Team Managers, and appointed Project Assurance roles, and agree them with the Project Board

- manage business and project risks, including the development of contingency plans

- liaise with programme management if the project is part of a programme

- liaise with programme management or related projects to ensure that work is neither overlooked nor duplicated

- take responsibility for overall progress and use of resources, and initiate corrective action where necessary

- be responsible for change control and any required configuration management

- report to the Project Board through Highlight Reports and stage assessments

- liaise with the Project Board or its appointed Project Assurance roles to assure the overall direction and integrity of the project

- agree technical and quality strategy with appropriate members of the Project Board

- prepare the Lessons Learned Report

- prepare any Follow-on Action Recommendations required

- prepare the End Project Report

- identify and obtain any support and advice required for the management, planning and control of the project

- be responsible for project administration

- liaise with any suppliers or account managers.

A.6   Team Manager

A.6.1   General

The use of this role is optional. The Project Manager may find that it is beneficial to delegate the authority and responsibility for planning the creation of certain products and managing a team of specialists to produce those products. There are many reasons why it may be decided to employ this role. Some of these are the size of the project, the particular specialist skills or knowledge needed for certain products, geographical location of some team members, and the preferences of the Project Board.

The Team Manager's prime responsibility is to ensure production of those products defined by the Project Manager to an appropriate quality, in a timescale and at a cost acceptable to the Project Board. The Team Manager reports to and takes direction from the Project Manager.

The use of this role should be discussed by the Project Manager with the Project Board and, if the role is required, planned at project initiation time.

A.6.2 Specific responsibilities

The specific responsibilities of the Team Manager are to:

- prepare plans for the team's work and agree these with the Project Manager
- receive authorisation from the Project Manager to create products (Work Package)
- manage the team
- direct, motivate, plan and monitor the teamwork
- take responsibility for the progress of the team's work and use of team resources, and initiate corrective action where necessary within the constraints laid down by the Project Manager
- advise the Project Manager of any deviations from plan, recommend corrective action, and help prepare any appropriate Exception Plans
- pass products which have been completed and approved in line with the agreed Work Package requirements back to the Project Manager
- ensure all Project Issues are properly reported to the person maintaining the Issue Log
- ensure the evaluation of Project Issues which arise within the team's work and recommend action to the Project Manager
- liaise with any Project Assurance roles
- attend any stage assessments as directed by the Project Manager
- arrange and lead team checkpoints
- ensure that quality controls of the team's work are planned and performed correctly
- maintain, or ensure the maintenance of, team files
- identify and advise the Project Manager of any risks associated with a Work Package
- ensure that such risks are entered on the Risk Log
- manage specific risks as directed by the Project Manager.

A.7   Project Assurance

A.7.1   General

The Project Board members do not work full-time on the project, therefore they place a great deal of reliance on the Project Manager. Although they receive regular reports from the Project Manager, there may always be the questions at the back of their minds, 'Are things really going as well as we are being told?', 'Are any problems being hidden from us?', 'Is the solution going to be what we want?', 'Are we suddenly going to find that the project is over-budget or late?' There are other questions. The supplier may have a quality assurance function charged with the responsibility to check that all projects are adhering to the quality system.

All of these points mean that there is a need in the project organisation for an independent monitoring of all aspects of the project's performance and products. This is the Project Assurance function.

To cater for a small project, PRINCE starts by identifying these Project Assurance functions as part of the role of each Project Board member. According to the needs and desires of the Project Board, any of these assurance responsibilities can be delegated, as long as the recipients are independent of the Project Manager and the rest of the Project Management Team. Any appointed assurance jobs assure the project on behalf of one or more members of the Project Board.

It is not mandatory that all assurance roles are delegated. Each of the assurance roles which is delegated may be assigned to one individual or shared. The Project Board decides when an assurance role needs to be delegated. It may be for the entire project or only part of it. The person or persons filling an assurance role may be changed during the project at the request of the Project Board. Any use of assurance roles needs to be planned at initiation stage, otherwise resource usage and costs for assurance could easily get out of control.

There is no stipulation on how many assurance roles there must be. Each Project Board role has assurance responsibilities. Again, each project should determine what support, if any, each Project Board role needs to achieve this assurance.

For example, the supplier's work standards may be certificated under ISO 9001. A requirement of the certification is that there will be some form of quality assurance function which is required to monitor the supplier's work. Some of the Senior Supplier's assurance responsibilities may be delegated to this function. Note that they would only be delegated. The Project Board member retains accountability. Any delegation should be documented. The quality assurance could include verification by an external party that the Project Board is performing its functions correctly.

Assurance covers all interests of a project, including all business, user and supplier.

Project Assurance has to be independent of the Project Manager, therefore the Project Board cannot delegate any of its assurance responsibilities to the Project Manager.

A.7.2 Specific responsibilities

The implementation of the assurance responsibilities needs to answer the question 'What is to be assured?' A list of possibilities would include:

- maintenance of thorough liaison throughout the project between the supplier and the customer
- user needs and expectations are being met or managed
- risks are being controlled
- adherence to the Business Case
- constant reassessment of the value-for-money solution
- fit with the overall programme or company strategy
- the right people being involved
- an acceptable solution is developed
- project remains viable
- the scope of the project is not 'creeping up' unnoticed
- focus on the business need is maintained
- internal and external communications are working
- applicable standards are being used
- any legislative constraints are being observed
- the needs of specialist interests, e.g. security, are being observed
- adherence to quality assurance standards.

It is not enough to believe that standards will be obeyed. It is not enough to ensure that a project is well set up and justified at the outset. All the aspects listed above need to be checked throughout the project as part of ensuring that it remains consistent with and continues to meet a business need and that no change to the external environment affects the validity of the project.

A.8   Project Support

A.8.1 General

The provision of any project support on a formal basis is optional. It is driven by the needs of the individual project and Project Manager. Project support could be in the form of advice on project management tools, guidance and administrative services, such as filing, the collection of actuals, to one or more related projects. Where set up as an official body, project support can act as a repository for lessons learned, and a central source of expertise in specialist support tools.

One support function which must be considered is that of configuration management. Depending on the project size and environment, there may be a need to formalise this, and it quickly becomes a task with which the Project Manager cannot cope without support. See Chapter 9 on configuration management for details of the work.

A.8.2 Specific responsibilities

The following is a suggested list of tasks covering both administration and advice.

Administration

These tasks would include:

- administer change control
- set up and maintain project files
- establish document control procedures
- compile, copy and distribute all project management products
- collect actuals data and forecasts
- update plans
- administer the quality review process
- administer Project Board meetings
- assist with the compilation of reports.

Advice

These tasks would involve:

- specialist knowledge (e.g. estimating, risk management)
- specialist tool expertise (e.g. planning and control tools, risk analysis)
- specialist techniques
- standards.

APPENDIX B   PRINCE PRODUCT DESCRIPTIONS

This appendix contains Product Outlines for the management and quality products that would be produced in a normal PRINCE2 project. As with other elements of PRINCE2, the formality of their creation and use will depend on the needs of the project (and the Project Manager). They are outlines, rather than Product Descriptions, because they lack some of the standard headings and content of a Product Description, such as format, skills required and to whom allocated. These may vary from project to project, so no attempt has been made to define what a specific project will need.

B.1   General quality criteria

Below is a list of general quality criteria which can be applied to most documents. Rather than repeat them for each suitable product, they are listed here once. Attach them to Product Descriptions as required.

General quality criteria demand that:

- documents are clear and concise
- documents are accurate
- the coverage is comprehensive
- the composition matches that stated in the Product Description
- the grammar and spelling are correct
- the product meets the defined standard
- the product is on the required form
- the product reflects accurately the information contained in/required by the derivation material
- the information is at the correct level for the readership
- the information is free from jargon which is unknown or unexplained to the readership
- the information is provided under every expected heading
- the information provided under each heading is appropriate to that heading
- input has been provided from all the relevant parties
- the document's summary/conclusions are consistent with the body of the report
- the product fulfils its stated purpose
- the product is delivered on time
- the contents match the contents page

- the product's author is clearly indicated
- the distribution list is provided and correct
- the version number is clearly indicated and correct
- the header and footer information matches the required standard.

B.2   Acceptance criteria

B.2.1 Purpose

A definition in measurable terms of what must be done for the final product to be acceptable to the customer and staff who will be affected.

B.2.2 Composition

This will vary according to the type of final product. The list below contains suggestions for criteria:

- target dates
- major functions
- appearance
- personnel level required to use/operate the product
- performance levels
- capacity
- accuracy
- availability
- reliability (mean/maximum time to repair, mean time between failures)
- development cost
- running costs
- security
- ease of use
- timings.

B.2.3 Derivation

Acceptance criteria are derived from the Project Brief and the Senior User.

B.2.4 Quality criteria

All criteria should be measurable. Each criterion should be individually realistic. The criteria as a group should be realistic, e.g. high quality, early delivery and low cost may not go together.

B.3   Business Case

B.3.1 Purpose

The purpose of the Business Case is to document the justification for the undertaking of a project based on the estimated cost of development and the anticipated business benefits to be gained.

The Business Case is used to say why the forecast effort and time will be worth the expenditure. The Project Board will monitor the on-going viability of the project against the Business Case.

B.3.2 Composition

The Business Case should contain:

- reasons
- benefits
- cost and timescale
- investment appraisal.

B.3.3 Derivation

Information for the Business Case is derived from:

- the Project Mandate/Project Brief (reasons)
- the Project Plan (costs)
- the customer.

B.3.4 Quality criteria

Questions raised should include:

- Can the benefits be justified?
- Do the cost and timescale match those in the Project Plan?
- Are the reasons for the project consistent with corporate or programme strategy?

B.4   Checkpoint Report

B.4.1   Purpose

The purpose of the Checkpoint Report is to report at a frequency defined in the Stage Plan the status of work for each member of a team.

B.4.2   Composition

The composition of the Checkpoint Report should include:

- date held
- period covered
- follow-ups from previous reports
- activities during the period
- products completed during the period
- quality work carried out during the period
- actual or potential problems or deviations from plan
- work planned for the next period
- products to be completed during the next period.

B.4.3   Derivation

The Checkpoint Report is derived from:

- verbal reports from team members
- Stage or Team Plan
- a previous checkpoint.

B.4.4   Quality criteria

- Is every item in the Stage or Team Plan for that period covered?
- Is every team member working to an agreed schedule?
- Is every team member's work covered?
- Is an update included on any unresolved problems from the previous report?

B.5   Communication Plan

B.5.1 Purpose

The Communication Plan identifies all parties who require information from the project and those from whom the project requires information. The plan defines what information is needed and when it should be supplied.

B.5.2 Composition

The Communication Plan should comprise:

- list of interested parties (such as user groups, suppliers, stakeholders, Quality Assurance, Internal Audit)
- information required by each identified party
- identity of the information provider
- required frequency of communication
- method of communication.

B.5.3 Form(at)

The Communication Plan should be set to the defined site standard for reports with the above content.

B.5.4 Derivation

The Communication Plan should be derived from:

- the Project Board
- other stakeholders
- the Project Brief
- the Project Initiation Document
- the Project Quality Plan
- the Project Approach.

B.5.5 Quality criteria

- Have all the listed derivation sources been checked?
- Has the timing, content and method been agreed?
- Has a common standard been agreed?
- Has time for the communications been allowed for in the Stage Plans?

B.5.6 Quality method

Informal quality review between Project Manager and those identified in the Communication Plan.

B.6   End Project Report

B.6.1 Purpose

The report is the Project Manager's report to the Project Board on how well the project has performed against its Project Initiation Document. This includes the original planned cost, schedule and tolerances, the revised Business Case and final version of the Project Plan. The Project Board may pass it on to corporate or programme management.

B.6.2 Composition

The End Project Report should describe:

- the achievement of the project's objectives
- performance against the planned target time and cost
- the effect on the original Project Plan and Business Case of any changes which were approved
- final statistics on change issues received during the project
- the total impact of approved changes
- statistics for all quality work carried out
- any planned Post Project Review date.

B.6.3 Derivation

The End Project Report is derived from:

- the updated Project Plan
- the Project Initiation Document
- Issue Log.

B.6.4 Quality criteria

- Does the report describe the impact of the approved changes on the Project Initiation Document?
- Does the report cover all the benefits which can be assessed at this time?

■ Does the quality work done during the project meet the quality expectations of the customer?

B.7   End Stage Report

B.7.1 Purpose

The purpose of the End Stage Report is to give a summary of progress to date, the overall project situation and sufficient information to ask for a Project Board decision on what to do next with the project.

The Project Board uses the information in the End Stage Report to decide what action to take with the project: approve the next stage, ask for a revised next Stage Plan, amend the project scope, or stop the project.

B.7.2 Composition

The End Stage Report should comprise:

■ current Stage Plan with all the actuals
■ Project Plan outlook
■ Business Case review
■ risk review
■ Project Issue situation
■ quality statistics
■ Project Manager's report on any events which affected stage performance.

B.7.3 Derivation

Information for the report is obtained from:

■ the Stage Plan and actuals
■ the next Stage Plan (if appropriate)
■ the updated Project Plan
■ the embryo Lessons Learned Report
■ data from the Quality Log
■ completed Work Package data.

B.7.4 Quality criteria

■ Does it clearly show stage performance against the plan?

- Were any abnormal situations described, together with their impact?
- Do any appointed Project Assurance roles agree with the report?

B.8   Exception Report

B.8.1   Purpose

An Exception Report is produced when costs and/or timescales for an approved Stage Plan are forecast to exceed the tolerance levels set. It is sent by the Project Manager in order to appraise the Project Board of the adverse situation.

An Exception Report will normally result in the Project Board asking the Project Manager to produce an Exception Plan.

B.8.2   Composition

The Exception Report comprises:

- a description of the cause of the deviation from the Stage Plan
- the consequences of the deviation
- the available options
- the effect of each option on the Business Case, risks, project and stage tolerances
- the Project Manager's recommendations.

B.8.3   Derivation

The information for an Exception Report may come from:

- current Stage Plan and actuals
- Issue Log
- Risk Log
- checkpoints
- Project Board advice about an external event that affects the project.

B.8.4   Quality criteria

- Does the current Stage Plan accurately show the status of budget and schedule?
- Are the reason(s) for the deviation stated?
- Are both technical and resource plans included in the Exception Plan?

B.9   Highlight Report

B.9.1 Purpose

The purpose of the Highlight Report is to provide the Project Board with a summary of the stage status at intervals defined by them.

The Project Board uses the report to monitor stage and project progress. The Project Manager also uses it to advise the Project Board of any potential problems or areas where the Project Board could help.

B.9.2 Composition

The Highlight Report comprises:

- date
- period covered
- budget status
- schedule status
- products completed during the period
- actual or potential problems
- products to be completed during the next period
- Project Issue status
- budget and schedule impact of the changes.

B.9.3 Derivation

Information for the Highlight Report is derived from:

- checkpoints
- Issue Log
- Stage Plan
- Risk Log.

B.9.4 Quality criteria

- Is it an accurate reflection of checkpoint information?
- Is it an accurate summary of the Issue Log?
- Is it an accurate summary of plan status?
- Are any potential problem areas highlighted?

B.10   Issue Log

B.10.1   Purpose

The purpose of the Issue Log is to:

- allocate a unique number to each Project Issue
- record the type of Project Issue
- be a summary of the Project Issues, their analysis and status.

B.10.2   Composition

The Issue Log provides:

- Project Issue number
- Project Issue type (Issue, Request For Change, Off-Specification)
- author
- date identified
- date of last update
- description
- status.

B.10.3   Derivation

Project Issues may be raised by anyone associated with the project at any time.

B.10.4   Quality criteria

- Does the status indicate whether action has been taken?
- Are the Project Issues uniquely identified, including to which product they refer?
- Is access to the Issue Log controlled?
- Is the Issue Log kept in a safe place?

B.11   Lessons Learned Report

B.11.1   Purpose

The purpose of the Lessons Learned Report is to pass on any lessons which can be usefully applied to other projects.

The data in the report should be used by a corporate group, such as quality assurance, who are responsible for the quality management system, in order to refine, change, improve the standards. Statistics on how much effort was needed for products can help improve future estimating.

B.11.2 Composition

The Lessons Learned Report should list:

- what management and quality processes:
  - ☐ went well
  - ☐ went badly
  - ☐ were lacking
- a description of any abnormal events causing deviations
- an assessment of technical methods and tools used
- an analysis of Project Issues and their results
- recommendations for future enhancement or modification of the project management method
- useful measurements on how much effort was required to create the various products
- statistics on how effective quality reviews and other tests were in error trapping (e.g. how many errors were found after products had passed a quality review or test).

B.11.3 Derivation

Information for the report is derived from:

- observation and experience of the processes
- Quality Log
- completed Work Packages
- Stage Plans with actuals.

B.11.4 Quality criteria

- Has every management control been examined?
- Is input to the report being done, minimally, at the end of each stage?
- Is every specialist technique included?
- Are statistics of the success of quality reviews and other types of test used included?
- Are details of the effort taken for each product given?

B.12   Off-Specification

B.12.1 Purpose

To document any situation where a product is failing, or is forecast to fail, to meet its specification.

B.12.2 Composition

The Off-Specification should provide:

- date
- Issue Log number
- class
- status
- description of the fault
- impact of the fault
- priority assessment
- decision
- allocation details, if applicable
- date allocated
- date completed.

B.12.3 Derivation

Normally will come from the supplier, but can be raised by anyone associated with the project.

B.12.4 Quality criteria

- Is the fault logged in the Issue Log?
- Is there an accurate description of the problem?

B.13   Post Project Review

B.13.1 Purpose

The purpose of the Post Project Review is to find out:

- whether the expected benefits of the product have been realised

- if the product has caused any problems in use.

Each expected benefit is assessed for the level of its achievement so far, and any additional time needed for the benefit to materialise.

The use of the product may have brought unexpected side effects, beneficial or adverse. These are documented with explanations of why these were not foreseen. Recommendations are made to realise or improve benefits, or counter problems.

B.13.2 Composition

The Post Project Review should list:

- achievement of expected benefits
- unexpected benefits
- unexpected problems
- user reaction
- follow-on work recommendations.

B.13.3 Derivation

The expected benefits should have been defined in the Project Brief and expanded in the Project Initiation Document.

General comments should be obtained about how the users feel about the product. The type of observation will depend on the type of product produced by the project, but examples might be its ease of use, performance, reliability, contribution it makes to their work, and suitability for the work environment.

B.13.4 Quality criteria

- Are all the benefits mentioned in the Project Brief and Business Case covered?
- Is each achievement described in a tangible, measurable form?
- Is a recommendation made in any case where a benefit is not being fully met, a problem has been identified, or a potential extra benefit could be obtained?
- Is the review conducted as soon as the benefits and problems can be measured?

B.14   Product Checklist

B.14.1   Purpose

The purpose of the Product Checklist is to list the items to be produced within a Stage Plan, together with key status dates. It is used by the Project Board to monitor progress.

B.14.2   Composition

The Product Checklist should provide:

- plan identification
- product names (and reference numbers if appropriate)
- columns for planned and actual dates for:
  - ☐ draft ready
  - ☐ quality check
  - ☐ approval.

B.14.3   Derivation

The Product Checklist is extracted from the Stage Plan.

B.14.4   Quality criteria

- Do the details and dates match those in the Stage Plan?
- Are the product names the same as those that appear in the PFD and bar chart?

B.15   Product Description

B.15.1   Purpose

The purpose of the Product Description is to describe a required product in sufficient detail such that the approach and effort required for its construction can be understood and estimated.

It should also describe the quality expected of the finished product to the person who will create it and anyone who will be asked to check that the finished product possesses those qualities.

B.15.2 Composition

The Product Description should provide:

- purpose
- composition
- derivation
- format
- quality criteria
- quality review method
- checklist identity (where appropriate)
- provided by (if from an external source).

B.15.3 Derivation

The Product Description is obtained from:

- the user
- anyone invested with assurance responsibility for that type of product.

B.15.4 Format

The Product Description should be set out in a one- or two-page document.

B.15.5 Quality criteria

- Is the composition of the description correct?
- Is the composition field complete and down to a level which allows the effort to be estimated?
- Are the quality criteria expressed in measurable form?

B.16   Project Brief

B.16.1 Purpose

The purpose of the Project Brief is to provide a full and firm foundation for the initiation of the project.

The contents are extended and refined into the Project Initiation Document that is the working document for managing and directing the project.

The Project Brief is a key document in its own right. It is the basis of the Project Initiation Document, which gives the direction and scope of the project and forms the 'contract' between the Project Management Team and corporate or programme management. Any significant change to the material contained in the Project Brief will thus need to be referred to corporate or programme management.

B.16.2 Composition

The following is a suggested list of contents, which should be tailored to the requirements and environment of each project.

- Project Definition, explaining what the project needs to achieve. It will contain:
  - ☐ background
  - ☐ project objectives
  - ☐ project scope
  - ☐ outline project deliverables and/or desired outcomes
  - ☐ any exclusions
  - ☐ constraints
  - ☐ interfaces
- Outline Business Case
  - ☐ description of how this project supports business strategy, plans or programmes
  - ☐ reason for selection of this solution
- customer's quality expectations
- acceptance criteria
- any known risks.

If earlier work has been done, the Project Brief may refer to the document(s) containing useful information, such as the outline Project Plan, rather than include copies of them.

B.16.3 Derivation

It is developed from the Project Mandate supplied at the start of the project, produced by the process Starting Up a Project (SU), and accepted via Authorising Initiation (DP1).

If the project is part of a programme, the programme should provide the Project Brief. In such circumstances it will not have to be derived from a Project Mandate.

If no Project Mandate is provided, the Project Manager has to generate the Project Brief from scratch in discussions with the customer and users.

B.16.4 Quality criteria

- Does it accurately reflect the Project Mandate?

- Does it form a firm basis on which to initiate a project (Initiating a Project (IP))?

- Does it indicate how the customer will assess the acceptability of the finished product(s)?

B.17   Project Initiation Document

B.17.1 Purpose

The purpose of the Project Initiation Document is to define the project, to form the basis for its management and the assessment of overall success.

There are two primary uses of the document:

- to ensure that the project has a sound basis before asking the Project Board to make any major commitment to the project

- to act as a base document against which the Project Board and Project Manager can assess progress, change management issues, and on-going viability questions.

B.17.2 Composition

The following are the base elements of information needed to direct correctly and manage a project. They cover the following fundamental questions about the project:

- what a project is aiming to achieve

- why it is important to achieve it

- who is going to be involved in managing the process and what their responsibilities are

- how and when it is all going to happen.

The information will be held in various ways and the following contents should not be read as a list of contents for one document, but should rather be seen as the information needed in order to make the initiation decisions:

- background, explaining the context of the project, and how we have arrived at the current position of requiring a project

- Project Definition, explaining what the project needs to achieve. Under this heading may be:

  - ☐ project objectives

  - ☐ defined method of approach

  - ☐ project deliverables and/or desired outcomes

- ☐ project scope
- ☐ constraints
- ☐ exclusions
- ☐ interfaces
- ■ assumptions
- ■ initial Business Case, explaining why the project is being undertaken
- ■ project organisation structure, explaining who will be on the Project Management Team
- ■ Project Quality Plan (see the separate Project Quality Plan Product Outline)
- ■ initial Project Plan, explaining how and when the activities of the project will occur (for details of the Project Plan content, see the separate Product Outline)
- ■ Project Controls, laying down how control is to be exercised within the project, and the reporting and monitoring mechanisms which will support this
- ■ exception process
- ■ initial Risk Log, documenting the results of the risk analysis and risk management activities
- ■ contingency plans, explaining how it is intended to deal with the consequences of any risks which materialise
- ■ project filing structure, laying down how the various elements of information and deliverables produced by the project are to be filed and retrieved.

B.17.3 Derivation

The Project Initiation Document is derived from:

- ■ supplier's project management standards
- ■ customer's specified control requirements.

Much of the information should come from the Project Mandate, enhanced in the Project Brief. Initially the Project Initiation Document will be completed during the initiation stage. Parts of it, such as the Project Plan and Business Case, may be updated and refined by each pass through the process Managing Stage Boundaries (SB) and will finally be archived as part of the process Closing a Project (CP).

B.17.4 Quality criteria

- ■ Does the document correctly represent the project?
- ■ Does it show a viable, achievable project which is in line with corporate strategy, or overall programme needs?
- ■ Is the project organisation structure complete, with names and titles?

- Have all the roles been considered?

- Does it clearly show a control, reporting and direction regime which is implementable, and appropriate to the scale, business risk and business importance of the project?

- Is the project organisation structure backed up by agreed and signed job descriptions?

- Are the relationships and lines of authority clear?

- Does the project organisation structure need to say to whom the Project Board reports?

- Do the controls cover the needs of the Project Board, Project Manager and Team Managers?

- Do the controls satisfy any delegated assurance requirements?

- Is it clear who will administer each control?

B.18   Project Issue

B.18.1 Purpose

Project Issue is a generic term for any matter which has to be brought to the attention of the project, and requires an answer. After receiving a unique reference number, Project Issues are evaluated in terms of impact on the product, effort and cost. The Project Manager may make a decision on what action to take, or the Project Issue may be referred to the Project Board. A Project Issue may be a:

- Request For Change

- Off-Specification

- question

- statement of concern.

B.18.2 Composition

The Project Issue should provide:

- author

- date

- issue number

- description of the issue

- priority

- impact analysis

- decision

- signature of decision maker(s)

- date of decision.

B.18.3 Derivation

Anyone may submit a Project Issue. Typical sources are users and specialists working on the project.

B.18.4 Quality criteria

- Is the problem/requirement clear?
- Have all the implications been thought out?
- Has the Project Issue been correctly logged?

B.19   Project Mandate

B.19.1 Purpose

The information in the mandate is used to trigger the process Starting up a Project (SU). It should contain sufficient information to identify at least the prospective Executive of the Project Board and indicate the subject matter of the project.

It will be used to create the Project Brief.

B.19.2 Composition

The actual composition of a Project Mandate will vary according to the type and size of project and also the environment in which the mandate is generated. The project may be a completely new piece of work which has just arisen, it may be the outcome of an earlier investigation or it may be part of a larger programme.

The following list contains suggested contents, and should be tailored to suit the specific project. It includes:

- authority responsible
- background
- project objectives
- scope
- constraints
- interfaces
- quality expectations
- outline Business Case (reasons)

- reference to any associated documents or products
- an indication of who are to be the project Executive and Project Manager
- the customer(s), user(s) and any other known interested parties.

If the mandate is based on earlier work, there may be other useful information, such as an estimate of the project size and duration, a view of the risks faced by the project.

B.19.3 Derivation

A Project Mandate may come from anywhere, but it should come from a level of management which can authorise the cost and resource usage.

B.19.4 Quality criteria

- Is the level of authority commensurate with the anticipated size, risk and cost of the project?
- Is there sufficient detail to allow the appointment of an appropriate Executive and Project Manager?
- Are all the known interested parties identified?
- Does the mandate describe what is required?

B.20   Project Plan

B.20.1 Purpose

A mandatory plan which provides a statement of how and when a project's objectives are to be achieved, by showing the major products, activities and resources required on the project.

It provides the Business Case with planned project costs, and identifies the management stages and other major control points.

It is used by the Project Board as a baseline against which to monitor project progress and cost stage by stage.

B.20.2 Composition

This product forms part of the Project Initiation Document and will contain the following:

- Plan Description, giving a brief description of what the plan covers
- project prerequisites, containing any fundamental aspects which must be in place at the start of the project, and which must remain in place for the project to succeed

- external dependencies
- planning assumptions
- Project Plan, covering:
  - ☐ project level Gantt or bar chart with identified management stages
  - ☐ project level Product Breakdown Structure
  - ☐ project level Product Flow Diagrams
  - ☐ project level Product Descriptions
  - ☐ project level activity network
  - ☐ project financial budget
  - ☐ project level table of resource requirements
  - ☐ requested/assigned specific resources.

B.20.3 Derivation

The Project Plan is refined from the outline Project Plan in the Project Brief during the process Initiating a Project (IP). It can also be modified during the process Updating a Project Plan (SB2).

B.20.4 Quality criteria

- Is the plan achievable?
- Does it support the rest of the Project Initiation Document?

B.21   Project Quality Plan

B.21.1 Purpose

The Project Quality Plan is part of the Project Initiation Document. Its purpose is to define how the supplier intends to deliver products which meet the customer's quality expectations and the supplier's quality standards.

B.21.2 Composition

The Project Quality Plan should list:

- quality responsibilities
- reference to any standards that need to be met
- key product quality criteria
- the quality control and audit processes to be applied to project management

- quality control and audit process requirements for specialist work
- change management procedures
- Configuration Management Plan (see Chapter 9 on configuration management for explanation of the term)
- any tools to be used to ensure quality.

B.21.3 Derivation

The Project Quality Plan is derived from:

- customer's quality expectations
- corporate or programme quality management system (QMS).

B.21.4 Quality criteria

- Does the plan clearly define ways in which the customer's quality expectations will be met?
- Are the defined ways sufficient to achieve the required quality?
- Are responsibilities for quality defined up to a level which is independent of the project and Project Manager?
- Does the plan conform with the corporate quality policy?

B.22 Quality Log

B.22.1 Purpose

The purpose of the Quality Log is to:

- issue a unique reference for each quality check planned
- act as a pointer to the quality check documentation for a product
- act as a summary of the number and type of quality checks held.

The log summarises all the quality checks which are planned/have taken place, and provides information for the End Stage and End Project Reports, as well as the Lessons Learned Report.

B.22.2 Composition

For each entry in the log there should be a:

- reference number
- product

- planned date
- actual date
- result
- number of action items
- target sign-off date
- actual sign-off date.

B.22.3 Derivation

A blank Quality Log is created as part of IP1, Planning Quality.

The first entries are made when a quality check or test is entered on a Stage Plan. The remaining information comes from the actual performance of the check. The sign-off date is when all corrective action items have been signed off.

B.22.4 Quality criteria

- Is there a procedure that will ensure that every quality check is entered on the log?
- Has responsibility for the log been allocated?

B.23   Request For Change

B.23.1 Purpose

The purpose of a Request For Change is to request a modification to a product or an acceptance criterion as currently specified.

B.23.2 Composition

A Request For Change should give:

- date
- Issue Log number
- class
- status
- description of the proposed change
- impact of the change
- priority assessment
- decision
- allocation details, if applicable

- date allocated
- date completed.

B.23.3 Derivation

Anyone connected with the project can propose a Request For Change.

B.23.4 Quality criteria

- Is the source clearly identified?
- Is the request logged in the Issue Log?
- Has an accurate description of the requested change been supplied?
- Is the benefit of making the change clearly expressed and, where possible, in measurable terms?

B.24   Risk Log

B.24.1 Purpose

The purpose of the Risk Log is to:
- allocate a unique number to each risk
- record the type of risk
- be a summary of the risks, their analysis and status.

B.24.2 Composition

The Risk Log should provide:
- risk number
- risk type (business, project, stage)
- owner
- date identified
- status
- date of last update
- likelihood
- severity
- description
- countermeasure(s).

B.24.3 Derivation

Business risks may have been identified in the Project Brief and should be sought during project initiation. There should be a check for any new business risks every time the Risk Log is reviewed, minimally at each End Stage Assessment. The Project Board has the responsibility to check constantly external events for business risks.

Project risks are sought during project initiation when the Project Plan is being created. Some project risks may have been identified in work which led up to the Project Mandate. Project risks should be reviewed every time the Risk Log is reviewed, minimally at each End Stage Assessment.

Risks to a Stage Plan should be examined as part of the production of that plan. They should be reviewed at each time of plan update.

B.24.4 Quality criteria

- Does the status indicate whether action has been taken or is in a contingency plan?
- Are the risks uniquely identified, including to which project they refer?
- Is access to the Risk Log controlled?
- Is the Risk Log kept in a safe place?
- Are activities to review the Risk Log in the Stage Plans?

B.25   Stage Plan

B.25.1 Purpose

The Stage Plan is used as the basis for project management control throughout the stage. To summarise:

- it identifies all the products which the stage must produce
- it provides a statement of how and when a stage's objectives are to be achieved, by showing the deliverables, activities and resources required
- it identifies the stage's control and reporting points and frequencies
- it provides a baseline against which stage progress will be measured
- it records the stage tolerances
- it specifies the quality controls for the stage and identifies the resources needed for them.

B.25.2 Composition

This product will contain the following:

- Plan Description, covering:
  - ☐ a brief description of what the plan covers
  - ☐ a brief description of the planned approach
- Quality Plan, outlining:
  - ☐ the quality control methods to be used
  - ☐ the resources to be used in each quality test or check
- plan prerequisites, containing any fundamental aspects which must be in place at the start of the stage, and which must remain in place for the plan to succeed
- external dependencies
- tolerances (time and budget)
- how the plan will be monitored and controlled
- reporting method
- planning assumptions
- graphical plan, covering:
  - ☐ diagram showing identified resources, activities, start and end dates (usually a Gantt or bar chart)
  - ☐ Product Breakdown Structure
  - ☐ Product Flow Diagram
  - ☐ activity network
  - ☐ financial budget
  - ☐ table of resource requirements
- risk assessment
- Product Descriptions for the major products.

B.25.3 Derivation

The Stage Plan is refined from the Project Plan during the process Planning a Stage (SB1). It is based on resource availability and is updated during Assessing Progress (CS2). It may be modified during Reviewing Stage Status (CS5) and Taking Corrective Action (CS7). An Exception Plan will have the same format as a Stage Plan.

B.25.4 Quality criteria

- Is the plan achievable?

- Do any Team Managers involved in its operation believe that their portion is achievable?
- Does it support the Project Plan?
- Does it take into account any constraints of time, resources and budget?
- Has it been taken down to the level of detail necessary to ensure that any deviations will be recognised in time to react appropriately (e.g. within the stage tolerances, and within the activity 'floats')?
- Has it been developed according to the planning standard?
- Does the Stage Plan contain activities and resource effort to review the Issue Log?

B.26   Work Package

B.26.1   Purpose

A Work Package is a set of information about one or more required products collated by the Project Manager and its purpose is formally to pass responsibility for work or delivery to a Team Manager or team member.

B.26.2   Composition

This product will vary in content, and indeed in degree of formality, depending on circumstances. Where the work is being conducted by a team working directly under the Project Manager, the Work Package may be a verbal instruction, although there are good reasons for putting it in writing, such as avoidance of misunderstanding and providing a link to performance assessment. Where the work is being carried out by a supplier under a contract and the Project Manager is part of the customer organisation, there is a need for a formal written instruction in line with standards laid down in that contract.

Although the content may vary greatly according to the relationship between the Project Manager and the recipient of the Work Package, it should cover:

- Product Description(s)
- techniques/processes/procedures to be used
- interfaces to be satisfied by the work
- interfaces to be maintained during the work
- quality checking arrangements
- reporting requirements.

B.26.3 Derivation

There could be many Work Packages authorised during each stage. The Project Manager creates a Work Package from the Stage Plan. After the initial start of a stage subsequent Work Packages will be triggered by the process Reviewing Stage Status (CS5). Changes to the Stage Plan brought about when performing the process Taking Corrective Action (CS7) may also trigger the authorisation of new Work Packages.

B.26.4 Quality criteria

- Is the required Work Package clearly defined and understood by the assigned resource?
- Is there a Product Description for the required product(s) with clearly identified and acceptable quality criteria?
- Does the Product Description match up with the other Work Package documentation?
- Are standards for the work agreed?
- Are the defined standards in line with those applied to similar products?
- Have all necessary interfaces been defined?
- Do the reporting arrangements include the provision for exception reporting?

APPENDIX C
PROJECT FILING STRUCTURE

Every project produces products that require filing. This may be:

- storage of finished products until they can be handed over to the customer on completion of the project
- storage of intermediate products, waiting to be used to contribute to a later product
- storage of information that may be needed for audit purposes
- documentation of decisions made during the project.

It makes a lot of sense if a site or company adopts one filing structure for all its projects, so that as staff move from one project to another, they will quickly be able to retrieve or store documents for the new project. This is a suggested filing system to be used for projects.

There are three types of file in PRINCE:

- management
- specialist
- quality.

C.1 Management files

These comprise:

- a project file
- a stage file for each stage.

C.1.1 Project file

This has the following sections:

- Organisation

  The project organisation chart and signed job descriptions.
- Plans

  The Project Plans. This should include all versions developed, not only the one approved as part of the Project Initiation Document. All the various components of each version should be kept (such as Product Breakdown Structures, Product Flow Diagrams) with clear identification of their date, version number and reasoning, such as change of assumptions, scope, resource availability and so on.

  The Project Plan should be updated at least at the end of each stage.

- Business Case

  Versions of the Business Case, updated at each stage end or when Exception Plans are created.

- Risk Log

  Updated details of all identified risks, their status and countermeasures.

- Control

  Copies of project initiation and closure documents.

C.1.2 Stage files

These have more sections than the project file.

- Organisation

  Stage organisation, details of team members. These should reflect all work assignments, achievements and the Project or Team Manager's assessment of the work performance.

- Plans

  Copies of the Stage Plans, any Team Plans and Exception Plans, updated with actual information as available.

- Control

  Copies of Work Package Authorisations, Checkpoint Reports, Highlight Reports, Exception Reports, the End Stage Assessment plus any exception assessments held.

- Daily Log

  A diary of events, problems, questions, answers, informal discussions with Project Board members, and actions for the stage.

- Correspondence

  Copies of management correspondence or other papers associated with the stage.

C.2   Specialist file(s)

This contains all the specialist products of the project, and is the centre of the configuration management activity. There will be a log with identification details of every product and a reference to its physical location. This method should also cater for sensitive products that may have to be filed separately.

If an Off-Specification is raised about a product, a copy of the Off-Specification form is filed with the product in this section of the filing.

C.2.1 Specialist correspondence

There may also be a need to create this section of the specialist file, where correspondence or external documents cannot be specifically related to one product. The section should have its own log of entries, showing cross-references to the products concerned.

C.3 Quality file

The objective of a quality file is to permit an audit at any time of the quality work being done and to confirm adherence to quality standards. There is one quality file which runs through the whole project and is not divided into stages. It has three major divisions: Product Descriptions, Quality Checks and Project Issues.

C.3.1 Product Descriptions

This section should contain the master copy of all Product Descriptions. There should be a Product Description for every major product in the project.

C.3.2 Quality checks

It is useful to head this section with a log giving a number to each check, the type of check or test (e.g. quality review), the product and date. This is a quick reference to see or show how many checks have been held in a particular stage and a guide to where the appropriate documentation can be found.

The sub-division of the quality section will depend on the type(s) of check or test being made. The filing for quality reviews, for example, should have separate sections for:

- invitations
- result notifications
- action lists.

C.3.3 Project Issues

This should have a log at the front, the Issue Log, to facilitate sequential numbering and to record the status and allocation. The subject of Project Issues is covered fully in Chapter 10 which deals with change control.

APPENDIX D   CHECKLISTS

Checklists are provided to Reviewers at a quality review to confirm that deliverables are produced using the requisite standards. They can also be useful to the person creating the product in the first place. They should be derived from the Product Descriptions and chosen methodology, tools and techniques.

The following generic checklists are designed to give guidance. They do not claim to be a 'tick list' of every expected finding or event, but do provide a basis from which to start.

D.1   Problem definition checklist

■ Is the correct person defining the problem?

■ Has the describer a sufficient grasp of the problem background, environment and future actions planned?

■ Is it the real problem or only a symptom?

■ Is there a danger of solving a small problem, which is in fact part of a larger problem, whose solution would be a totally different one?

■ Is the author merely describing the problem or attempting to define the solution?

■ Have the major business functions required been identified?

■ Look at the objectives:

☐ Are they clearly defined?

☐ What is mandatory?

☐ Have the 'wants' been prioritised?

■ Was the correct level of management authority obtained when considering quality expectations, cost, delivery date and other acceptance criteria?

■ Why do they want a new product? What is wrong with the current product? Are the reasons real or imaginary?

■ Are the limits of the project clearly defined?

■ Is the scope compatible with the project's objectives?

■ Have any constraints been identified? Are they genuinely necessary? Are they reasonable?

■ Have any restrictions on the use of specific equipment been defined?

■ Do the terms of reference make clear the number, location and grade of users for the product, and the type of environment?

■ Have any known future additional requirements been defined?

- Have acceptance criteria been defined? Are they prioritised? Are they all stated in measurable terms?
- Is there a specific duration to the need for the new product?
- Is it clear if (and which) other departments must be consulted?
- Have any required data already been gathered?
- Is the expected time frame feasible and necessary? Have the necessary project stages been provisionally identified?
- Is the problem definition understood?
- Is it acceptable without modification?

D.2   Acceptance criteria checklist

- Are all criteria expressed in measurable terms?
- Have all levels of user, operator and those responsible for support and maintenance been canvassed for their criteria?
- Do the user criteria cover cost in terms of:
  - ☐ development costs
  - ☐ operating costs
  - ☐ maintenance costs?
- Do the user criteria cover performance in terms of:
  - ☐ major functions to be performed
  - ☐ ease of use
  - ☐ reliability
  - ☐ flexibility
  - ☐ quality of user staff required
  - ☐ documentation required
  - ☐ availability of the product
  - ☐ durability/ruggedness
  - ☐ error reporting and recovery
  - ☐ mean time between failures
  - ☐ mean time to repair
  - ☐ security?
- Do the user criteria cover capacity in terms of:
  - ☐ volumes to be processed by the product

☐ frequency of use?

■ Has each criterion been identified as either 'mandatory' or 'desirable'?

■ Have the desirable criteria been given a priority rating?

D.3   Project start-up checklist

■ Have the Executive and Project Manager been appointed?

■ Has the Project Management Team been designed?

■ Have the other members of the Project Board been appointed?

■ Has consideration been given to the allocation of assurance roles? Have internal audit and quality assurance been considered when allocating assurance roles?

■ Do agreed, documented and signed job descriptions exist for all appointed members of the Project Management Team?

■ Is there a Project Brief which meets its Product Description?

■ Has a Risk Log been created?

■ Has the Initiation Stage Plan been prepared?

■ Has the project's approach to a solution been defined?

■ Were all reasonable alternative approaches considered and fully evaluated?

■ Does the Business Case cover at least the reasons for the project?

D.4   Planning checklist

■ Has sensible time been allowed for each task?

■ Is there a sensible sequence of tasks?

■ If any tasks overlap, is this justified? Is the amount of overlap reasonable?

■ Do certain consecutive tasks need a gap between them?

■ Is there a specific target date for the plan imposed from client/management? If so, does the plan meet this deadline?

■ What contingency has been included in the plan? Does the amount of contingency relate to the level of experience of the team in doing this type of project?

■ Is the timescale chosen for the plan reasonable when compared to the duration of the plan?

■ Is there a description of the plan?

■ Has the plan been examined for any assumptions made in its preparation?

■ Have any prerequisites been identified?

If it is a Stage Plan:

- Have resources been identified against every task?
- Has sensible resource availability been defined? Has allowance been made for the fact that human resources are not 100% efficient?
- Has sufficient time been allowed to carry out the impact analysis on Project Issues?
- Are there adequate quality reviews? Has sufficient time been allowed for preparation and the quality review? Has any time been allowed for revision of the product after quality review?
- Has enough time been allowed for project management activities, e.g. updating the plan, work allocation, reporting, checking on critical specialist activities, monitoring risks?
- Have resources been overscheduled on this project?
- Are any resources also doing other work outside this project, where the combination of the jobs will over-schedule them?
- If any over-scheduling is deliberate, is it reasonable, and has it been agreed with the resource?
- Has the workload for each resource been balanced in a reasonable way?
- Have the resources been consulted about their part in the plan? Do they agree that they can reasonably be expected to attain their targets?
- Has the expected quality level of the work been identified to the resources? Does a Product Description exist for all the products to be produced in the plan?
- Is any special people preparation required for the next stage (e.g. training etc.)?
- Has the plan been broken down to sufficiently small tasks (maximum five days) that it will be possible to control accurately against it?

D.5   Project initiation checklist

- Has the Project Brief been confirmed? Has this been discussed and agreed informally between Project Manager and Project Board?
- Has any strategy documentation affecting the project been obtained and studied?
- Is there any other background material which would be of use?
- Has the correct level of management authority been obtained when considering cost, delivery date and other acceptance criteria?
- What justification, benefits and expenditure have been considered?
- Are any suggested benefits/savings valid?
- Are benefits/savings defined in a way which will be measurable after the product is delivered?
- Has a risk assessment been carried out?

- Are all high-scoring risks covered by a countermeasure?

- Have business risks been considered as well as project risks?

- What business situations might cause a significant change in direction during the project?

- Has the project management organisation structure been defined and agreed with all members?

- Have job descriptions been tailored and signed off?

- Do Product Descriptions exist? Have they been done in sufficient detail to assist the planning process? Have the quality criteria been carefully thought out? Were users involved in creating the Product Descriptions, particularly the quality criteria?

- Is there a Project Plan? Is there a description with it?

- Are the planning assumptions and prerequisites clearly stated?

- Have any external dependencies been identified?

- Is there a Project Quality Plan? Does it meet the requirements of the customer's quality expectations? Are quality responsibilities clearly defined and satisfactory in the eyes of the customer?

- Has the Project Plan been broken down into stages that offer a sensible balance between adequate control and management by exception for the Project Board?

- Is the reporting frequency and content acceptable to the Project Board?

- Have tolerances been defined for the project? Do the tolerances on time and cost match with the time frame of the project and its risk situation?

- Have scope and quality tolerances been discussed with the Project Board, especially if the time and cost tolerances are tight?

- Is there a clear definition of how change control will be exercised?

- Is the escalation procedure for forecast deviations clearly defined?

- Has the approach to configuration management been established?

- Is there a next Stage Plan?

- Has the End Stage Assessment been arranged?

(See also the next three checklists.)

D.6   Analysis of benefits checklist

Here are a number of headings under which savings and/or benefits might be obtained:

- staff reduction, e.g. salary + overheads X no. of staff saved = saving

- saving bureau costs

- work now to be done by lower grades

- lower equipment rental charges
- disposal of current equipment (or share of its costs)
- lower communication costs
- paper saving
- less wastage
- new method of generating income
- competitive advantage leading to increased business
- increased profit margins
- avoidance of penalties or fines
- faster response/turnaround time:
  - ☐ Does faster response mean cash gets to the bank faster?
  - ☐ Does faster response mean that invoices are sent earlier?
  - ☐ Does faster response save business which otherwise would be lost?
  - ☐ Does faster response mean fewer transactions need price (or other data) corrections later?
  - ☐ Might a faster decision save the company from some problems?
- facilities not available at present:
  - ☐ Does a new facility offer a clerical saving (clerical staff cost X number of annual repetitions = value)?
  - ☐ Does this new facility prevent a staff increase?
  - ☐ Will current staff be able to do other work with the time saved?
- removal of repetitive work
- staff time saving: will some old tasks no longer be required, freeing up staff to tackle other work (which can be costed)?
- more accurate and timely management information for decision-making:
  - ☐ Does the more timely information show up theft or staff error which can be remedied before it is too late? How much time is saved and what is the amount involved?
  - ☐ What are the major management decisions being made using output from this product? How much earlier can these now be made? What is the value of that time saving? Is it a once-only saving or a regularly recurring saving?
- earlier management decisions bring forward a product launch date (this would be an example of a once-only saving)
- saving on current maintenance contracts.

D.7   Development costs checklist

This could include:

- user staff training
- development staff training
- preparation of training material
- equipment purchase/rental
- communication costs
- documentation costs
- development/contractual staff costs
- consultancy costs
- travel costs
- installation costs
- maintenance costs
- inflation.

D.8   Running costs checklist

This could include:

- training new/replacement user staff
- stationery and consumables
- input preparation
- output handling
- rentals/amortisation/processing cost
- maintenance/enhancement of product
- software support
- hardware maintenance
- back-up
- disaster recovery precautions
- operations staff
- costs of possible staff regrading
- communications costs
- inflation.

D.9   Requirements definition checklist

- Has the Stage End Product, the User Specification, been produced to standards?
- Is the purpose and scope of the study still in line with the Problem Definition and feasibility study?
- Is the summary of the existing product a true reflection of the facts gathered in the feasibility study?
- Does the summary of functional requirements highlight the major facilities?
- Does the outline new product show how the functional requirements will be met?
- Does the outline new product show sufficient timing information to satisfy the user that performance criteria will be met?
- Is the justification a true copy of the facts presented in the feasibility study? Have any changes been explained and justified?
- If there are any short-term recommendations, are these clearly highlighted?
- Is there sufficient information on data volumes, trends and performance needs made available for the design stages?
- Where are there requirements to interface with other products? Are any modifications planned for those products which will affect this new product?
- Were all relevant user views and needs covered by the interviews carried out? Have any relevant users' needs been assumed? What method was used to ensure that the interviewees confirmed that the correct facts were documented?
- Is there a measurable acceptance criterion for each required function? Is there a minimum acceptance level for each one? Is it clear how each acceptance criterion will be tested?
- Has the acceptance strategy been defined, together with the necessary resourcing for such tests?

D.10   Quality review checklist

D.10.1   Preparation

- Have invitations been sent? Did the invitation contain all the necessary information?
- Has adequate preparation time been allowed between sending the invitation and holding the review? Did this allow for post, travel, complexity, other work?
- Did the invitation make the roles known to the attendees? (Chairman, Scribe, Reviewer, Producer, standards)?

D.10.2 Review

- Is time wasted in repeating what was in the preparation documentation?
- Have the attendees prepared a list of questions?
- Did the Chairman merge and prioritise the questions?
- Was the available time divided according to the number of questions and their priorities?
- Were all Reviewers involved?
- Were any dead-end arguments identified and either resolved or made into action points?
- Was any attempt by Reviewers at redesign spotted and stopped?
- Was the Scribe allowed enough time to document action points?
- Were read-backs of action points taken from the Scribe? Was this done at the end and at suitable moments during the review?
- Were corrective actions allocated?
- Were people identified to check each corrective action?
- Was a decision reached on the overall result of the review?
- Was the Project Manager informed of the result?

D.10.3 Follow-up

- Were the action points followed up and all checked off?
- Were all attendees informed of the final sign-off?
- Was the Project Manager informed of the final sign-off?
- Was all the review documentation filed correctly?

APPENDIX E GLOSSARY

Acceptance criteria
A prioritised list of criteria, which the final product(s) must meet before the customer will accept them. They should be defined as part of the Project Brief and agreed between customer and supplier no later than the project initiation stage. They should be in the Project Initiation Document.

Activity network
A flow diagram showing the activities of a plan and their interdependencies. The network shows each activity's duration, earliest start and finish times, latest start and finish times and float. See also critical path.

Baseline
A snapshot; a position or situation which is recorded. Although the position may be updated later, the baseline remains unchanged and available as a reminder of the original state and as a comparison against the current position.

Benefit
A positive outcome, quantified or unquantified, expected as a result of delivering the end product of a project; a justification for the project investment

Business Case
Information that describes the justification for setting up and continuing a PRINCE project. It provides the reasons (answers the question 'why?') for the project. It is updated at key points throughout the project.

Change authority
A group to which the Project Board delegate responsibility for the consideration of Requests For Change. The change authority is given a budget and can approve changes within that budget

Change budget
The money allocated to the change authority to be spent on authorised Requests For Change.

Change control
The procedure to ensure that the processing of all Project Issues is controlled, including the submission, analysis and decision-making.

Checkpoint meeting
A team level, time-driven review of progress.

Checkpoint Report
A progress report of the information gathered at a checkpoint meeting, which is sent from a team to the Project Manager, and provides reporting data as defined in the Project Initiation Document.

Concession	An Off-Specification which is accepted by the Project Board without corrective action.
Configuration management	A discipline, normally supported by software tools, which gives management precise control over its assets (e.g. the products of a project), covering identification, control, status accounting and verification of the products.
Contingency plan	A plan which provides an outline of decisions and measures to be taken if defined circumstances, outside the control of a PRINCE project, should occur.
Corporate and corporate body	Used to describe any company, government department, corporation, charitable body which is involved in a project. It can be a customer for the end results, supplier of specialist skills or deliverables, assurance or auditing body. The word is used to avoid confusion particularly between the public and private sectors.
Critical path	The path through a planning network linking those activities with the minimum float (usually zero). Any slippage of an activity on the critical path will affect the end date of the network.
Customer	The person or group who commissioned the work and will benefit from the end results.
End Project Report	A report sent from the Project Manager to the Project Board, which confirms the handover of all deliverables, provides an updated Business Case, and an assessment of how well the project has done against its Project Initiation Document.
End Stage Assessment	The review by the Project Board and Project Manager at the end of a stage of the End Stage Report to decide whether to approve the next Stage Plan (unless the last stage has now been completed). According to the size and criticality of the project, the review may be formal or informal. The approval to proceed should be documented as an important management product
End Stage Report	A report sent by the Project Manager to the Project Board at the end of each management stage of a PRINCE project. This provides information about the project performance during the Stage and the project status at stage end.
Exception	A situation where it can be forecast that there will be a deviation beyond the tolerance levels agreed between Project Manager and Project Board or between Project Board and corporate or programme management.

Exception assessment	This is a form of the process DP3, Authorising a Stage or Exception Plan, where the Project Board considers whether to accept an Exception Plan.
Exception Plan	A plan which follows an Exception Report. For a Stage or Team Plan exception it covers the period from the present to the end of the current stage. If the exception is at a project level, the Project Plan would be revised.
Exception Report	A report that describes an exception, provides an analysis and options for the way forward and identifies a recommended option. It is sent from the Project Manager to the Project Board.
Executive	The chairman of the Project Board, representing the customer.
Follow-on Action Recommendations	A report which can be used as input to the process of creating a Business Case/Project Mandate for any follow-on PRINCE project, and/or for recording any follow-on instructions covering incomplete products or outstanding issues. It also sets out proposals for Post Project Review of the project's deliverables.
Highlight Report	Report from the Project Manager to the Project Board on a time-driven frequency on stage progress.
Host organisation	The Business Case holder, the corporate body who will be the primary beneficiary of the project's results, and who typically will be responsible for the overall conduct of the project.
Issue Log	A log of all issues and change requests raised during the project, showing details of each issue, its evaluation, what decisions about it have been made and its current status.
Lessons Learned Log	A folder or similar grouping where any lessons learned during a project are stored until the close, when they are put into a formal Lessons Learned Report.
Lessons Learned Report	A report that describes the lessons learned in undertaking a PRINCE project and which includes statistics from the quality control of the project's management products. It is approved by the Project Board then held centrally for the benefit of future projects.
Off-Specification	Something that should be provided by the project, but currently is not (or is forecast not to be provided). This might be a missing product or a product not meeting its specification.
Post Project Review	One or more reviews held after Project Closure to determine if the expected benefits have been obtained.

PRINCE2	A methodology that supports some selected aspects of project management. The acronym stands for Projects in Controlled Environments.
PRINCE project	A project whose product(s) can be defined at its start sufficiently precisely as to be measurable against pre-defined metrics and which is managed according to the PRINCE2 methodology.
Process	That which must be done to bring about a particular outcome, in terms of information to be gathered, decisions to be made and results which must be achieved.
Producer	This role represents the creator(s) of a document that is the subject of a quality review. Typically it will be filled by the person who has produced the product, or who led the team responsible.
Product	Any output from a project. PRINCE distinguishes between management products (which are produced as part of the management of the project), specialist products (which are those products which make up the final deliverable) and quality products (which are produced for or by the quality process). A product may itself be a collection of other products.
Product-based planning	Product-based planning is a three-step diagrammatic technique leading to a comprehensive plan based on creation and delivery of required outputs. The technique considers prerequisite products, quality requirements and the dependencies between the products.
Product Breakdown Structure	A hierarchy of all the products to be produced during a plan.
Product Description	A description of a product's purpose, composition, derivation and quality criteria. It is produced at planning time, as soon as the need for the product is identified.
Product Flow Diagram	A diagram showing the sequence of production and interdependencies of the products listed in a Product Breakdown Structure.
Project	A temporary organisation which is created for the purpose of delivering one or more business products according to a specified Business Case.
Project Assurance	The Project Board's responsibilities to assure itself that the project is being conducted correctly.

Project Brief	A description of what the project is to do; a refined and extended version of the Project Mandate, which has been agreed by the Project Board and which is input to Project Initiation.
Project closure notification	Advice from the Project Manager to inform the host location that the project resources can be disbanded and support services, such as space, equipment and access, demobilised.
Project Initiation Document (PID)	A logical document whose purpose is to bring together the key information needed to start the project on a sound basis; and to convey that information to all concerned with the project.
Project Issue	A term used to cover both general issues and change requests raised during the project. Project Issues can be about anything to do with the project. They cover questions, suggestions, Requests For Change and Off-Specification.
Project management	The planning, monitoring and control of all aspects of a project and the motivation of all those involved in it to achieve the project objectives on time and to the specified cost, quality and performance.
Project Management Team	A term to represent the entire management structure of Project Board, Project Manager, plus any Team Managers and Project Assurance roles.
Project Manager	The person given the authority and responsibility to manage the project on a day-to-day basis to deliver the required products within the constraints agreed with the Project Board.
Project Mandate	A document, created externally to the project, which forms the terms of reference and is used to start up a PRINCE project.
Project Plan	A high-level plan showing the major products of the project, when they will be delivered and at what cost. An Initial Project Plan is presented as part of the Project Initiation Document. This is revised in later versions as information on actual progress appears. It is a major control document for the Project Board to measure actual progress against expectations.
Project Quality Plan	The definition of key quality criteria and quality control and audit processes to be applied to project management and technical work in the PRINCE project. It will be part of the text in the Project Initiation Document.

Project records   A collection of all approved management and specialist products and other material, which is necessary to provide an auditable record of a PRINCE project.
NB This does *not* include working files.

Project start-up notification   Advice to the host location that the project is about to start and requesting any required project support services.

Project Support Office   A group set up to provide certain administrative services to the Project Manager. Often the group provides its services to many projects.

Quality   The totality of features and characteristics of a product or service which bear on its ability to satisfy stated and implied needs.

Quality management system (QMS)   The complete set of quality standards, procedures and responsibilities for a site or organisation.

Quality review   A quality review is an inspection with a specific structure, defined roles and procedure designed to ensure a document's completeness and adherence to standards. The participants are drawn from those with an interest in the document and those with the necessary skills to review its correctness. An example of the checks made by a quality review is 'Does the document match the quality criteria in the Product Description?'

Quality system   See Quality management system.

Request For Change   A means of proposing a modification to the current specification of the product required. It is one type of Project Issue.

Reviewer   A person asked to review a product which is the subject of a quality review.

Risk Log   A document which provides identification, estimation, impact evaluation and countermeasures for all risks to a PRINCE project. It should initially be created externally to the project and be developed during the life of the project.

Senior Supplier   The Project Board role which provides commitment of the resources involved in the production of the project's deliverable(s) and is responsible for the quality of those products.

Senior User   A member of the Project Board, accountable for ensuring that user needs are specified correctly and that the solution meets those needs. Also commits any user resources required by the plans.

Stage

A division of the project for management purposes. The Project Board approve the project to proceed one stage at a time.

Supplier

Supplier is defined as the group or groups responsible for the supply of a project's products.

Tolerance

The permissible deviation above and below a plan's estimate of time and cost without escalating the deviation to the next level of management. Separate tolerance figures should be given for time and cost

User(s)

The person or group who will use the final deliverable(s) of the project.

Work Package

The set of information relevant to the creation of one or more products. It will contain the Product Description(s), details of any constraints on production such as time and cost, interfaces, and confirmation of the agreement between the Project Manager and the person or Team Manager who is to implement the Work Package that the work can be done within the constraints.

APPENDIX F TEMPLATES AND SAMPLE FORMS

This appendix contains samples of some of the management products defined by PRINCE2. The templates can be used as they are or they might form the basis for forms more suited to the reader's environment and needs. The samples are there to give an idea of how to complete the document.

PROJECT ISSUE

Project: Issue No:

Author   Date:

Situation Description

_____

_____

_____

Appraisal

Affected Products

_____

_____

_____

Technical Impact

_____

_____

_____

Business Case and Risk Impact

_____

_____

_____

Recommendation

_____

_____

_____

Date: Appraised by:

Action	Date:

Closed ☐   RFC ☐   O-S ☐ | Date:

QUALITY REVIEW INVITATION

Project: QR No:

To:

From:

Telephone:

You are cordially invited to attend the Quality Review of

Product: Configuration
                                                        Identity

Chairman:

Presenter:

Scribe:

Reviewers:

Attachments				Useful references
Product	☐		Checklist	
Product Description	☐		Standards	
Question List	☐		Other products	

Please return a copy of your Question List to

No later than

QUALITY REVIEW QUESTION LIST

Project: QR No:

Product: Date:

Question No.	Location	Description

QUALITY REVIEW ACTION LIST

Project:	QR No:
Stage:	Date:

Product:

Action No.	Description	Action By	Target Date	Checked By

Chairman's sign-off   Date:

QUALITY LOG

Ref. No.	Product	Planned date	Actual date	Result	No. of action items	Target sign-off date	Actual sign-off date

RISK LOG

Project:		Risk type:		Risk No.	
Date identified		Status		Date of last update	
Owner		Likelihood		Severity	

Description

Countermeasure

Project:		Risk type:		Risk No.	
Date identified		Status		Date of last update	
Owner		Likelihood		Severity	

Description

Countermeasure

Project:		Risk type:		Risk No.	
Date identified		Status		Date of last update	
Owner		Likelihood		Severity	

Description

Countermeasure

HIGHLIGHT REPORT

Project: **Stage:**

Period Covered: **Due Date:**

UNDERSPENT	ON BUDGET	OVERSPENT
£	☐	£

AHEAD	ON SCHEDULE	BEHIND
weeks	☐	weeks

PRODUCTS COMPLETED THIS PERIOD

-

ACTUAL or POTENTIAL PROBLEMS

-

PRODUCTS TO BE COMPLETED DURING THE NEXT PERIOD

-

PROJECT ISSUE STATUS

-

BUDGET AND SCHEDULE IMPACT OF THE CHANGES

Signature: **Date:**

Project/Team Manager

CHECKPOINT REPORT

Project:	**Stage:**

Date Held:	**Period Covered:**

Follow-ups from previous reports

Activities during this period

Products completed during this period

Quality work carried out during this period

Actual or potential problems or deviations from plan

Work planned for next period

Products to be completed during the next period

Signature: **Date:**

Project Brief

Background

Brief details of the history of previous work to the project.

Project Definition

Objectives

The Business Product to be delivered, planned end date and cost.

Scope

The scope of the deliverables; what is to be included; what is excluded which might have been thought to be in.

Constraints

Any specific constraints imposed by management, for example specific hardware and/or software which must be used; capability of end users.

Tolerance

Any previous forecast of cost and target date.

What project tolerance is allowed on end date and cost.

Quality expectations

The customer's quality expectations of the final product.

Business risks

Any known external risks to the project, e.g. government policy change. Any risks to the business caused by undertaking and delivering the project.

Business Case

Reasons for undertaking the project.

Any previous summary of the expected benefits to be gained from the end product.

Project Initiation Document

Background

Brief details of the history leading to the project.

Project Definition

Objectives

The key deliverables of the project, end date and cost.

Project deliverables

A list of the products to be delivered by the project.

Scope

The scope of the deliverables; what is to be included.

Constraints

Any specific constraints imposed by management, for example, target date; maximum budget; specific equipment which must be used; capability of end users.

Exclusions

What is excluded from the project's products which might have been thought to be in.

Acceptance criteria

The key criteria for judging the success of the project in priority order.

Method of approach

The general approach to providing the solution.

Interfaces

Identification of any projects or groups with which the project must interface.

Assumptions

Any key assumptions made by the Project Manager in deciding on the approach and in planning the project.

Initial Business Case

Reasons for the project, plus a summary of the expected costs and benefits.

Project organisation structure

A diagram of the Project Management Team with the names of the Project Board, Project Manager and Project Assurance Team.

Project Quality Plan

The standards and method(s) to be used to ensure the required level of quality and the quality responsibilities. If third parties will be providing products, there should be a note on how their product quality will be checked.

Initial Project Plan

Stages; their start and end dates; the major deliverables for each stage; the stage effort and cost.

Initial risk review

Any serious external risks and key internal risks to the project, their impact and proposed countermeasures.

Project controls

Controls

What controls will be used, such as ESAs, Work Packages, reviews of plans, Business Case and risks.

Tolerances

Indication of any previous assessment of project cost and time frame. A note of the tolerance margins agreed with the Project Board or passed down by senior management to the Project Board.

Reports

What reports are to be sent, from whom, to whom, and their frequency.

Configuration management

The Configuration Management Plan, showing what method will be used to keep track of the products, responsibilities, product naming convention to be used, and any link with operational configuration management for when the products are handed over.

Change control

How changes and requests for change will be handled.

Project filing structure

How and where will the project products and records be kept, plus any responsibilities.

Lessons Learned Report

Purpose

The purpose of this Lessons Learned Report is to pass on to other projects the useful lessons which have been learned from this project.

The Central Support Office, which is responsible for the site quality management system, should use the data in the report to refine, change and improve project management standards.

Project management

What went well

- Product-based Planning

   The use of product-based planning went well, especially in the planning workshops held with Service Delivery and the users. The planning process was easily understood, even by those completely new to planning of any kind. The involvement of Service Delivery at the planning stage of the project greatly improved their understanding and participation and contributed to much better co-operation between the development team and Service Delivery than has been the case in past projects.

- Project Initiation Document Workshop

   The workshop to produce a Project Initiation Document worked very well. It had a number of benefits:

   Taking the team off-site to a hotel was very cost- and time-effective. The Project Initiation Document was produced in two and a half days, whereas in some cases other projects have taken several weeks.

   Bringing together the team which represented developer, user and Service Delivery to create the Project Initiation Document created an excellent team spirit which lasted throughout the project. This is not the company's normal experience.

   The workshop's second objective was to give an overview of the project management method to those of the team unfamiliar with it. Apart from achieving the training objectives, this gave background and understanding of what the team was trying to achieve with the Project Initiation Document creation.

- Project Board

   The appointment and use of the Project Board contributed greatly to the success of the project. There was much more ownership by the Project Board than from senior management on a project not run under PRINCE2.

What went badly

- Product Descriptions

  The Product Descriptions produced originally were very bland and therefore virtually useless, particularly the quality criteria. A special exercise, using a PRINCE2 consultant had to be undertaken. The new Product Descriptions were much better (see above section).

- Quality reviews

  There were some early problems with the quality review technique. Some users failed to turn up as planned. Some of these sent a late apology, others forgot or said they were too busy when asked why they were absent. None sent in Question Lists. Another problem was Reviewers turning up who had clearly not read the product in advance. This caused delays and meant that the review could not be run according to the established procedure. Eventually these problems were sorted out through action from the Project Board, but much more 'progress chasing' to get Question Lists submitted in advance had to be done.

- Earned Value Analysis

  The attempt to use Earned Value Analysis was not a success. Many mistakes in the figures were made by the PSO through lack of training. The results, even when corrected, did not seem to be understood by the Project Board, again through a lack of training.

- Monthly Progress Meetings

  The insistence by the Project Board on monthly progress meetings was not very useful and these were stopped after three months.

Project management aspects lacking

- Business Case

  The lack of a recognised document structure and approach to the production of the Business Case caused unnecessary work. The idea of using the feasibility study Business Case did not work. It did not contain benefit measurements that can be applied in any Post Project Review.

- Technique Assessment

  Product-based planning was, apart from the problem with Product Descriptions mentioned under 'What Went Badly', very helpful. It eased the planning process and assisted in communication with the users. It also provided the right basis for Earned Value Analysis (but see the problems we had with that under the 'What Went Badly' heading).

- Support Tool Assessment

The use of Project Manager Workbench (PMW) was in the main very successful. The ability to consolidate the team plans at stage and project levels saved a great deal of planning and reporting time. The network planning part of the tool fitted in very well with the Product Flow Diagrams produced.

Problems were encountered in using the automatic scheduling feature. This must be used with care and users must be very disciplined in filing the plan before using this feature.

The PMW ability to create timesheets for individual progress reporting saved the project support function much time.

Abnormal events which affected operation of the project management method

The public announcement of an implementation date before the Project Plan had been produced had a serious effect on the project. When the Project Plan was produced it was obvious that not everything could be delivered by the published date. The project was pushed into an unnecessary exercise of de-scoping which was expensive and time-consuming because of the many project and product interdependencies which the project has.

Project Issue analysis

After some teething problems with users who were not accustomed to the procedure the Project Issue procedure worked very well. A breakdown of the Project Issues received and actions taken is given in the End Project Report.

Of the 33 Change Requests received, eight concerned functions that were known before the project and should have been part of the user requirements.

Whilst the volume of Project Issues was not great, they did require considerable time to decide on the course of action, mainly due to the busy work schedule of the Project Board members.

Recommendations

■ Product Descriptions

More and better training in the writing of Product Descriptions must be undertaken in order to make these useful products and not be seen as a bureaucratic waste of time. It would be worth our while to train up at least two people from the Central Support Office (CSO) as experts in writing Product Descriptions. In the medium and long term this is a more effective and cost-conscious solution than continuing to use a PRINCE2 consultant. (It should be said, however, that great value was gained by using the particular PRINCE2 consultant obtained for this work in this project.)

- Quality review

  Training in the quality review process should be given to all who may have to participate in these in a project.

- Business Case

  The company should adopt a standard way of producing and documenting the Business Case. We should either work to the Product Description given in the PRINCE2 manual, or get our Finance Department to create one for us.

- Earned Value Analysis

  If Earned Value Analysis is to be used, all concerned with creating and using the figures must be trained in the technique.

- Change Control

  Consideration should be given to the setting aside of a change budget for future projects to avoid having to go back to senior management for finance to cover required changes.

  This project was not a particularly volatile one in terms of user requirements. It was still difficult to get Project Board consensus on the implementation of change requests. Future projects should consider very carefully whether decisions (within constraints) on changes could be handed down to a lower level, e.g. a Change Control Board.

End Stage Report

The suggested structure for the End Stage Report is:

It should cover no more than two pages and should not be padded out with cover pages or paragraph numbering.

The first four sections are intended to bring the Project Board up to date with what happened in the stage and what effect this has had on the overall project . The second half of the report covers what is to happen next and what this will do to the overall project. This allows the Project Manager to explain any recovery actions or reaction to lessons learned from the interim Lessons Learned Report. It should cover the following topics:

Management summary

This should be a summary of the result of the stage, key points and events of the stage, any project impact, any unresolved problems and recommendations. Keep it brief because each of these points is expanded below.

All required products were delivered within the stage budget and schedule tolerances.

Stage details

Actual versus plan

This should be just a summary of two key facts, stage end date versus plan and stage cost versus plan.

Plan	Actual	Difference	Difference (%)	Tolerance (%)
£	£	± £		

Product status

All that is needed here is confirmation of products delivered. All products planned for the stage have been delivered to the agreed Quality Criteria.

Quality statistics

Details from the Quality Log, confirming that every product has been quality checked, numbers and type of check, and possibly the amount of effort spent on quality, if appropriate.

Project Issue status

This is best presented as a table, showing what has happened to each type of Project Issue:

	Brought forward	Received	Actioned	Rejected	Carried forward
PIR					
RFC					
OSR					

Problems

If any products have not been delivered or there are problems with any products, fuller details are required.

Project reassessment

Project Plan impact

To keep this brief, a small table can show the impact of the completed stages on the Project Plan.

	Original	Forecast	Difference	Difference (%)	Tolerance (%)
End date					
Project cost					

Business Case impact

This should identify any changes to the expected benefits caused by the completed stage or confirm that the stage results have not changed the expectations.

The stage results have not changed the Business Case figures.

Risk impact

This should describe any changes to the identified risks caused by the completed stage or any new risks which have arisen during the stage. This may lead to elements of the next Stage Plan which are specifically there to counter or take advantage of any change.

Lessons Learned Log

The LLR is formally presented to the Project Board at Project Closure. But if there any lessons to be learned from the completed stage which will affect the next stage these should be mentioned here as part of the Project Board's understanding of the next Stage Plan.

Next Stage Plan

Stage Plan

The actual next Stage Plan will be an annex to the report, so this is a summary with just enough information to make sense of the next section. It only needs to identify the major products of the stage, its start and end dates.

Stage resource requirements

A statement of the next stage resource requirements by type, showing quantities and cost.

Project forecast

Revised Project Plan

The same layout used to reflect the situation after the last stage can be used, but this time reflecting the next Stage Plan's impact.

Revised Business Case

This is a note of any major change to the Business Case caused by the next Stage Plan.

Revised risk review

This is a summary of any major change to risks caused by the next Stage Plan.

Recommendations

A statement that the Project Manager is looking for approval to proceed to the next stage, plus any special action which is desired of the Project Board.

APPENDIX G
RISK CATEGORIES

The categories below can be used as a starting point for identifying your organisation's main areas of risk in relation to projects or programmes.

Strategic/commercial risks

- under-performance to specification
- management will under-perform against expectations
- collapse of contractors
- insolvency of promoter
- failure of suppliers to meet contractual commitments; this could be in terms of quality, quantity, timescales or their own exposure to risk
- insufficient capital revenues
- market fluctuations
- fraud/theft
- partnerships failing to deliver the desired outcome
- the situation being non-insurable (or cost of insurance outweighs the benefit)
- lack of availability of capital investment.

Economic/financial/market

- exchange rate fluctuation
- interest rate instability
- inflation
- shortage of working capital
- failure to meet projected revenue targets
- market developments will adversely affect plans.

Legal and regulatory

- new or changed legislation may invalidate assumptions upon which the activity is based
- failure to obtain appropriate approval, e.g. planning, consent
- unforeseen inclusion of contingent liabilities
- loss of intellectual property rights
- failure to achieve satisfactory contractual arrangements

- unexpected regulatory controls or licensing requirements
- changes in tax or tariff structure.

Organisational management/human factors

- management incompetence
- inadequate corporate policies
- inadequate adoption of management practices
- poor leadership
- key personnel have inadequate authority to fulfil their roles
- poor staff selection procedures
- lack of clarity over roles and responsibilities
- vested interests creating conflict and compromising the overall aims
- individual or group interests given unwarranted priority
- personality clashes
- indecision or inappropriate decision-making
- lack of operational support
- inadequate or inaccurate information
- health and safety constraints.

Political/societal

- change of government policy (national or international), e.g. approach to nationalisation
- change of government
- war and disorder
- adverse public opinion/media intervention.

Environmental/Act of God (force majeure)

- natural disasters
- storms, flooding, tempests
- pollution incidents
- transport problems, including aircraft/vehicle collisions.

Technical/operational/infrastructure

- inadequate design
- professional negligence

- human error/incompetence
- infrastructure failure
- operation lifetime lower than expected
- residual value of assets lower than expected
- increased dismantling/decommissioning costs
- safety being compromised
- performance failure
- residual maintenance problems
- scope 'creep'
- unclear expectations
- breaches in security/information security
- lack or inadequacy of business continuity.

Interdependencies

Risks may have additional factors relating to them that increase the complexity of assessing your overall exposure to risk. Interdependencies is such a factor. It is essential to understand the interdependencies of risks and how they can compound each other. For example, a skills shortage combined with serious technical problems and a requirement to bring the delivery date forward are common examples of risks compounding. Interdependencies can occur at all levels and across different levels.

A project may have interdependencies with other projects. A project may be dependent upon a supplier delivering products or services that have a further interdependency upon another internal project delivering its objectives and so on in the supply chain. These need to be explicitly identified and assessed as part of the process of risk management. Interdependencies often cross different boundaries, such as ownership, funding, decision-making, organisational or geographical boundaries. You must be able to assess risk and communicate across these boundaries.

Relationship between benefit and delivery risks

Often the risk process is focused primarily on delivery rather than benefit. For example, changes to delivery dates, costs, quality etc. are not related back to the benefits. The drive to deliver may continue long after the potential benefits have been significantly reduced or lost. A common cause of this is that the owners of benefit objectives are not the same as the owners of delivery. Decisions taken with regard to delivery must be related back to benefit and vice versa.

Internal versus external risks

Much is made of the difference between internal and external risks. The major differences, however, relate to the ability to apply the risk process to them. Internal risks can be just as difficult to identify, assess and evaluate as external risks and thus just as complex to manage. The same broad principles of risk management apply to both.

INDEX

Page numbers in **bold** type refer to figures; those followed by an asterisk to glossary entries.